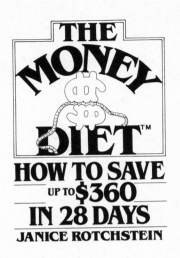

THE MONEY DIET™

HOW TO SAVE UP TO $360 IN 28 DAYS

JANICE ROTCHSTEIN

THE MONEY DIET

™

HOW TO SAVE
UP TO **$360**
IN 28 DAYS

JANICE ROTCHSTEIN

CROWN PUBLISHERS, INC.
NEW YORK

Published by Crown Publishers, Inc., One Park Avenue, New York,
New York 10016 and simultaneously in Canada by General Publishing
Company Limited

The Money Diet is a trademark of Janice Rotchstein

Manufactured in the United States of America

Library of Congress Cataloging in Publication Data
Rotchstein, Janice.
  The money diet.

  1. Consumer education. I. Title.
TX335.R7 1982   640.73   82-4980
ISBN: 0-517-543435   AACR2

Portions of the material contained in this book have been previously
published in a different form in *Redbook,* March 1981.

Please note: Costs for goods and services are subject to change, and therefore, the exact amounts of savings cannot be guaranteed. While all suggestions involving health and safety have been reseached with care, expert
advice should be sought and followed whenever possible.

Design by Joanna Nelson

10 9 8 7 6 5 4 3 2 1

First Edition

For Alan Ebert,
who encouraged me to write this book

For my parents,
who taught me the value of money

Acknowledgments

Developing, researching, compiling, tabulating, and writing *The Money Diet* wouldn't have been possible without the help of some very special people. I would like to thank:

Ann Pleshette Murphy, associate editor, and Sey Chassler, former editor in chief, *Redbook* magazine; it was with their shared support and blessings that I wrote this book, inspired by Ann. Her initial idea happily coincided with my interest in reducing personal expenses.

Aveline Brown, Kathy Chesworth, Charlie Escoffery, Joann Higgins, Anne Theis, and David Walston, the researchers who assisted me in gathering the national average prices used in this book. Together we canvassed some 500 stores and services—from fish markets to florists; private physicians to public health clinics; colleges and universities to high schools and elementary schools; catering manors to fast food stops; national chains to privately owned businesses; supermarkets to department stores; movie theaters to thrift shops —the list is endless. We surveyed prices in seven metropolitan areas: Chicago, Dallas, Los Angeles, Minneapolis–St. Paul, New York City, Seattle, and Washington, D.C. Those sections of the country were chosen to represent various parts of the U.S.—its diverse cities and suburbs—where we could focus on places where most people buy goods, be it on Main Street or in a shopping mall. It would be too space-consuming to include the names of all those who volunteered their time and price information, yet they know who they are, and we owe them our gratitude.

Fern Gale Estrow, Lisa Guck, and Kevin Meaney, who helped me research and compile national average costs and many money-saving ideas from friends, and such organizations, companies, associations, and governmental agencies as: American Automobile Association; American Cancer Society; American Druggist Bluebook; American-Electro-Dynamics Corp.; American Gas Association; American Heart Association; American Lamb Council; American Lung Association; American Meat Institute; American Telephone and Telegraph; American Water Works Association; Amtrak; Association of American Railroads; Atlantic Richfield, the Drive for Conservation; Beef Industry Council; Paul L. Bennett; Better Business Bureau; Better Vision Bureau; Bic Pen Corporation; Blue Cross/Blue Shield; B'Nai B'Rith Museum; Boyle-Midway, Inc.; *Bride's* magazine; California Table Grape Commission; Chilton Company; Chinese-American Restaurant Association; Church & Dwight Company; Colgate-Palmolive Company; Concord Grape Association; Con Edison; Consumer Credit Counseling Service; Consumer Industries Association, Consumer Electronics Group; Department of Consumer Affairs, New York City; Eastman Kodak; Edison Electric Institute; Barbara Ettorre; Rose Feifer; William Finnegan; Florida State Department of Citrus; General Electric; General Foods; General Mills; General Motors; General Telephone and Electronics Corporation; The Great Frame Up; Insurance Company of North America; Insurance Information Institute; International Apple Institute; Jewelry Industry Council; Kraft; Paul Lepelletiere; Bethel Leslie Magee Picture & Frame Company; Matthew Matheou; National Association of Greeting Cards; National Bridal Service Board; National Broiler Council; National Confectioners Association; National Institute of Health; National Public Radio; National Retail Merchants Association; National Turkey Federation; New York Public Library; New York State College of Human Ecology and the New York State College of Agriculture and Life Sciences, Statutory Colleges of the State University of Cornell University; New York State Energy Office; Oil Heat Institute of Long Island; Optical Manufacturers Association;

Acknowledgments

Parker Bros.; Pillsbury Company; Poultry and Egg Institute; Public Relations Society of America; L. Rabinowitz Hebrew Book Store; Roger Sammis; Shell Oil Company; Kenneth Singer, CPA; Society of Automotive Engineers; Sunkist Growers, Inc.; Supermarket Institute; Philip G. Taylor; 3M, Automotive Trades, Commercial Chemicals, and Household and Hardware Divisions and Eastern Public Relations; University of Arizona; U.S. Consumer Information Center; U.S. Department of Agriculture, Agricultural Marketing Services, Forest Service, Human Nutrition Information Service, and Science and Education Administration; U.S. Department of Commerce, National Bureau of Standards; U.S. Department of Energy, Energy Information Administration; U.S. Department of Health and Human Services; U.S. Department of Transportation, Federal Highway Administration Highway Statistics Division, Planning Services Branch, and the National Highway Traffic Safety Administration, Office of Public Affairs and Consumer Services; U.S. Energy Conservation Agency; U.S. Environmental Protection Agency; U.S. Postal Service; Village Cheese Shop, Bernardsville, N.J.; Anne Cayle Wallburg; Reed Wallburg; White House Office of the Special Assistant for Consumer Affairs; Delores Wolfe; and Richard E. Wolke, DVM, Ph.D.

Orna Reshef, who calculated the national average prices and savings that appear in this book. It was a demanding job and the final way we could reject any suggestion that didn't meet our expense-reducing standards. Orna also developed and refined a set of calculations that makes your figuring of any savings easier.

Nahum Waxman, my editor, who because of a personnel change at Crown Publishers, Inc., took over this book in its final months, but whose guidance and enthusiasm made it seem as if we had always worked together.

Kathy Robbins, my literary agent, who started it all by introducing me to Ann Pleshette Murphy, and whose wit and intelligence have helped me bring you *The Money Diet*.

Contents

1

Why This Book Saves You Money—Immediately

Within the next 28 days, I'm going to show you how to save up to:

$310 if you're single
$347 if you're a couple
$360 if you're a family of four

And should you be a variation of any of these—a single parent; family of five; separated supporter of several—don't worry. You'll still see how it's possible to trim your expenses and rival those totals.

That goes whether you're living in the city or the suburbs;

renting an apartment or buying a home; living on a salary or collecting a pension.

My promise is neither tinged with magic nor filled with malarkey. It doesn't condemn you to a life of scraping for every penny, or to taking on a host of money-saving projects that would bring Superman to his knees.

All I am suggesting is that you try following a simple 28-day money-spending plan that tells how you can purchase essential products and services less expensively, be they drugs or dry cleaning, food or fuel, entertainment or electricity.

Just as a weight-loss diet gives you a menu of meals to lose pounds, I'll be suggesting a menu of spending to help you reduce your expenses. Of course, with a weight-loss program you often have to give up your favorite foods. On my regimen you can have your cake and eat it too—often more cheaply than you're getting it for now. In essence, you don't have to forfeit your basic pleasures.

You see, I devised *The Money Diet* because I hate sacrifices almost as much as I hate paying high prices, which, in this economy, means that I used to have a constant headache. It had reached a point where my heating bill started me thinking about burning my furniture for fuel, and my weekly food budget made me want to take up serious fasting.

With so many bills depleting my bank balance, I began to wonder if I'd soon be living paycheck to paycheck.

Then a remarkable thing happened. (No, I didn't hear voices, experience a vision, or become a born-again spender.) At the supermarket I spied a package of six candy bars selling for $1.29.

Two things happened: I began to salivate, and I began to think, "Savings!" A little rapid mental division told me that each bar cost 22¢. That's when I started to ask myself, "Why am I paying 30¢ at the candy counter or vending machine whenever I buy a chocolate bar?" I could be devouring the identical treat for 8¢ less, and for each six bars bought in bulk I could realize a total savings of 51¢.

Then it happened again. There was a ten-pack of sugarless gum for $1.49, which translated to 15¢ per pack. I was used to paying 30¢ a pack. Although I've never been a whiz at math, I realized buying a packet of ten gum packages instead of the same number piecemeal meant another savings. This one was $1.51.

Since my parents didn't raise a dumb kid, I bought the two packages. As I stood on the checkout line among a battalion of depressed faces, the latest casualties of price increases, I was positively humming. With those purchases I had saved $2.02, *on the spot,* because that amount of cash wouldn't be paid out over the next several weeks for my candy bar and gum "breaks." By becoming my own "middleperson" I had trimmed my treat expenses.

That afternoon I realized there was life after inflation *and* without sacrifice, *if* you knew where, when, and how to spend your money. The bulk buy was a perfect example. I had successfully cut my costs *where* the items were sold in quantity, and *when* I was doing my weekly food buying at the supermarket. The *how* of it was learning to pay by the package. What I also liked was that I didn't exert extra energy, give up enjoying my munchies, or fork over a lot of cash.

As I began to think of other ways to economize I started focusing on things we need often and that consistently drain our wallets. Would it be possible, I wondered, to buy those necessities with the same ease with which I had purchased the candy and gum—and with such impressive savings?

Curious, I called one of my thrifty friends. She said, "Try thread instead of dental floss." I was delighted to find that a 50-yard spool of topstitching and buttonhole twist ran 60¢, while 50 yards of unwaxed extra-fine dental floss cost $1.50. By choosing the thread, I saved 90¢ *instantly,* and discovered that the sewing aid could be as effective as the floss recommended by my dentist.

I had found the additional keys to reducing expenses: you must either purchase what you need in a different manner or substitute less costly items that do as good a job. Building on those ideas, I started gathering hundreds of suggestions that would become *The Money Diet*. But before I would include any recommendation in the 28-day program, it had to meet three criteria:

• the product or service selected for purchase had to be something most of us need regularly;

• the execution of the idea couldn't demand excess energy or a lifestyle sacrifice;

• the savings had to be immediate.

While developing the final standard dealing with instant savings, I came upon *The Money Diet*'s philosophy: SAVE MONEY WHILE YOU SPEND IT. Hadn't I done exactly that when picking the thread rather than the dental floss? I *saved* 90¢ while *spending* cash on preventive dentistry.

Once I combined the diet's philosophy with its suggestions, I discovered that it would be easy to show you how to buy essential goods for less. So if you're game to make your dollars go further, then come on the 28-Day Plan with me. All you have to save is money.

2

Voices in Your Head—Learning to Talk Back

Since *The Money Diet* is simple to do, the only obstacle to its success could be one of those voices—the tempting whispers that can go off inside your head and prevent you from following through.

Before we cover the basics of the 28-Day Plan, let's zero in on what to listen for and how to talk back.

WHY START THE DIET THIS WEEK? It's soft and cajoling, but no other voice is more damaging than the one of procrastination. If you go along with it, you're apt to find yourself still another month down the line without having cut your expenditures. I suggest you reply: I'M TIRED OF BEING BROKE.

THE DIET WILL NEVER WORK. This is one of the worst mutterings from the depths, because it points unwaveringly toward failure. Ironically, if you ask, "Why won't it work?" the response will be: "It just won't." The best way to fight off this voice is to appreciate how each suggestion has been carefully chosen and documented as a money-saver. Then you can simply answer: LOOK AT THE PROOF.

I NEED THE BEST OF EVERYTHING. Watch out for this grumbler, to whom value means nothing; fashion-designer initials are everything, even on a T-shirt. So tell the voice you're about to educate it in the area of alternative buying, which doesn't mean sacrifices, but savings. Say firmly: I'M SECURE ENOUGH TO WEAR MY OWN INITIALS; I DON'T NEED SOMEBODY ELSE'S.

· WHAT WILL YOUR FRIENDS AND NEIGHBORS SAY? The insinuations of this accuser produce embarrassment. The fact is, if you tell your friends and neighbors what you're doing, they might even join you. So snap back at the voice: MONEY-SAVING IS IN THIS YEAR—EVERYBODY'S DOING IT.

LOOK AT THAT IDEA. IT ONLY SAVES YOU 30¢. THAT DOESN'T MEAN A THING. The answer is obvious: SAVINGS JUST KEEP ADDING UP.

CONVENIENCE IS MORE IMPORTANT THAN SAVING MONEY. If you're Jackie Onassis, you can afford this voice and live happily ever after. Since only one of us is, in fact, Jackie O., don't let this boaster get you. Most people who like expensive shortcuts end up with time on their hands—and broke. Send this sybarite packing: GIVE JACKIE MY BEST.

WHY NOT TAKE A VACATION FROM THE DIET? YOU CAN ALWAYS GO BACK TO IT. If you go along with this teaser's idea, you'll stop saving money, which is the reason you became interested in *The Money Diet* in the first place. Instead of allowing yourself to be defeated, why not react with: YOU TAKE A VACATION.

LET'S SPEND THAT EXTRA CASH YOU'RE NOW SAVING. Be careful of this voice. There will be more money in your wallet while you're dieting, and you can't let that tempt you. Just say, NO, THANKS. I LIKE HAVING A LITTLE EXTRA, AND I'M GOING TO HAVE A LOT MORE BY NOT GIVING IN.

GIVE UP. YOU'VE NEVER BEEN ABLE TO SAVE MONEY. This nasty soothsayer is related to THE DIET WILL NEVER WORK. Failure is its middle name, and if you listen to its words, it'll be yours too. Put this voice on hold, and when you see just how successful you've been, turn around and say: LOOK AT ME NOW. I'M A SAVER.

When you hear any of these "obstacles," I suggest you answer them in a good loud voice of your own—not in a public place, of course, unless there happen to be others on *The Money Diet* standing around. In that case, make your replies together, joining hands, and sing the "Hallelujah Chorus."

3

The Money Diet—
How It Works

Doesn't it seem like Uncle Sam is always calling us and asking, "How much money did you make?" Then he responds without taking a breath, "Good, send it all to me."

One way to snap back at "Sam," and at an economy that further diminishes our income is to increase the buying power of what we're left with each month. That can be accomplished on *The Money Diet*. Here's why:

HOW IT'S DONE: THE PLAN

The 28-day program revolves around a daily buying regimen that focuses on money-saving suggestions in five basic categories: Food, Transportation, Home Maintenance, Purchases (ranging from drugs to haircuts), and Entertainment.

I have selected these categories because they contain most of the types of items we shop for frequently, from hamburger meat to shampoo.

You'll find ideas in practically every category once a day, with two exceptions. One is Entertainment, which features tips only on Fridays, Saturdays, and Sundays, because that's when most of us spend our leisure dollars. The other is Transportation. During the final two weeks on the diet, I recommend that you car-pool to the office. Since that tip will reduce your daily fuel costs, I've listed the additional gasoline-saving techniques for those 14 days on the weekends.

Most of the daily diet entries save you money as soon as you complete them. Others don't pay off until the end of the four weeks, because you must repeat them regularly in order to receive their financial benefit.

An example would be lowering your thermostat a certain number of degrees or raising the air-conditioning dial to a higher level. For you to see a difference in the utility bill after you've finished the program, you have to keep the proposed setting for 28 days. To help you spot the ideas that must be carried out more than once or for the full diet, I've put the symbol **r** (repeat) at the beginning of the tip.

When you've completed the day's suggestions, merely total your savings. Then get ready for another day of recommendations and for more economizing.

That's the basics of the program.

HOW IT'S CALCULATED: THE $

The symbol **$** (Savings) follows most of the ideas and indicates what you could accrue by completing the tip. Each **$** is accompanied by a specific figure, be it 73¢, $3.84, or whatever, and it reflects the difference between two prices: (1) the cost of the product or service I suggest you buy, and (2) the one I say *not* to consider.

For example, I propose you substitute a half gallon of ice milk ($1.94) for the same amount of ice cream ($2.24) and realize a per half gallon $ of 30¢. The 30¢ is arrived upon by taking the two national average prices and subtracting one from the other ($2.24 − $1.94 = 30¢). It's no more complicated than that.

You'll notice in the example above the word *per*. It's there to help you calculate your savings. Should you purchase only a half gallon each month, your $ will be different from that of a person who eats a gallon. The *per* also assists you in adding up a tip's $ if you're on the diet with others.

An example is when I propose buying lamb without going broke. By eating lamb blade or round bone chops ($3.00 per pound) instead of loin chops ($4.05 per pound) the per serving $ is 52.5¢ or 53¢ (based on 2 servings per pound). Once you know the individual $, you just multiply it by the number of people on the diet to tally your $.

As you look at the prices I've quoted for the ice cream/ice milk and lamb choices, you're probably wondering, "How current are they?" My researchers gathered all the prices used in this book during the summer and fall of 1981. Each figure was the national average cost of products and services at that time. Since you and I know what's been happening to our economy, we both now realize my $ are conservative.

You're the key to updating them and to calculating your savings accurately. To determine your $, you'll have to note the cost, for example, of a half gallon of ice cream in your supermarket and subtract what you paid for the same amount of ice milk. That way you'll be able to compute how much you've decreased your snack or dessert bill.

I created the $, even though you have to figure your own, because I wanted to write a book that dealt with specifics. Too many "how-to" programs talk in either percentages or ranges. You've probably read them. "Do this and cut your gasoline bill 12%." Or "Try that, and you'll trim costs between $25.00 and $60.00." What do they mean to you? The only thing they really say is that the author wants to be safe, to not go out on a limb. I believe in taking a risk, if perhaps with a velvet safety net.

And that's what the $ is—a security blanket for you, a responsible risk for me. The $ is based on fact, and with it you can understand how I computed the savings.

My prices, then, are *guides,* and my $ is an *incentive. Neither should be used when compiling your personal savings.* Rather, they ought to give you a realistic goal to shoot for and to beat.

Although prices have changed since I wrote the diet, my suggestions will still save you cash. Even if the charges for the items increase, they will rise roughly in proportion to what they were when we researched them.

Take the idea about purchasing five disposable razors ($1.19) instead of as many refill blades ($2.28) for your razor. Should the cost of disposables go up, you can bet the price for refills will too. So although the savings you accrue will be different from what I've listed, you should still cut your expenditure for shaving aids.

Now you may be thinking, "Well, this is going to take a little time. I have to gather prices, do some arithmetic, keep a running total."

Don't give it a second thought. The math is simple, and in many cases calculations are provided in the text or in the Appendix to demonstrate how you can do your own numbers. As for gathering prices, it's true that when buying disposable razors you'll want to check what they're asking for refills. This should take only a few *seconds,* as both products are usually side by side. How many *minutes* of work go by before you earn $1.09 (which is what you save by selecting the disposables)?

There's another question you may have about *The Money Diet*'s **$**. Let's take the lamb example. You might say, "I don't eat meat, so I wouldn't benefit from that tip."

Or: "The cumulative four-week **$** is based on owning a car and cutting gasoline costs. That doesn't affect me."

The 28-Day Plan deals with what most of us use. If you're the exception, you won't save as much, and that's why I say "up to" in my final totals. On the other hand, you may be helped by the Bonus feature of the diet.

A Bonus suggestion follows at the end of each day. It can be substituted for any idea that you find doesn't fit your lifestyle *or* to further increase your **$**. This category has no assigned **$**, because it's generally a highly individual, highly variable savings-oriented activity, such as bartering to obtain products instead of exchanging cash.

HOW TO KEEP TRACK: THE CHART

At the end of this book, there are weekly charts that list in shorthand every tip that has been offered during the four weeks of the 28-day diet. Each calendar of ideas has been designed so you can cut it out of the book and put it up on your kitchen bulletin board or tape it on your refrigerator door. By putting the appropriate week's chart in a highly visible place, you'll be reminded of your commitment every time you pass by.

After each suggestion on the chart, there is a blank where you can write your savings. That way it'll be easy to keep an ongoing record of your personal **$** and then add them up at day's end.

As an incentive, you can compare your daily total with the minimum **$** I've tallied for:

Singles: a person who lives alone, owns a car, and is employed or on a pension;

Couples: two adults living together who have one car, no

children, and one of whom works or receives a retirement check;

Families of four: two adults, one of whom is employed full-time, and two children, ages six and eleven. The family has one car.

Now, should you not fit into any of these lifestyles, don't worry. Since each recommendation has been calculated on a per person or per item basis, it'll be easy for you to decide upon your $.

As you read through the diet, you'll notice that my daily totals for each lifestyle are conservative, because I normally tallied only one savings for every idea with the exception of Food and Entertainment, which I usually multiply by two for the couple, four for the family. This conservatism is most evident on those days when all three lifestyles save the same amount of money. I could have increased the $ for a couple or a family by assuming they might use more of a certain product than a single, but that's not my style as the assumption would load the totals and that's not my goal. I'd rather give you a minimum $ and let you decide if you can increase it.

This brings me to the last symbol, **+** (Plus). On some days I've listed several savings suggestions within one diet entry. To help you immediately spot which of the $ I've fed into my daily totals, I've placed the symbol **+** next to it.

These are the fundamentals of *The Money Diet*. The plan is no more complicated than counting calories.

4

The 28-Day Plan

As you start *The Money Diet,* you might want to review these Do's and Don'ts. They're designed to make your participation even more successful.

DO commit as many friends or members of the family as possible to the program. Group support will increase your savings.

DO read the complete plan through *before* you begin, so you can stock up on the necessary food items and know when to schedule the suggestions into your daily routine.

DO cut out the appropriate weekly chart as needed and put it in a highly visible place as a constant reminder of your diet days.

DON'T skip any sections or even one tip. Remember, if you

do, you're also skipping the chance to save money.

DO repeat those ideas coded with an **r** the exact number of times I've recommended so you'll receive the full dollar benefit.

DO figure your savings on the prices you're being charged, as opposed to using what I've listed with each explanation. Those costs and my **$** are merely guides and an incentive to help you realize how much you may be able to save.

DON'T be discouraged if your **$** is less than mine in a few instances. That can happen because my prices are national averages, and costs do vary from section to section of the country and at different times of year. You may well save more on other suggestions, and things will probably balance themselves out in the end.

DO consider doing the Bonus category as often as possible to extend your daily, weekly, and 28-day totals.

DO contact your utility and water company, before you begin the diet, to find out what you're charged per kilowatt-hour (kwh) (the basic unit of power supplied to and taken from an electrical current in one hour) and per gallon of water. That way you'll be able to calculate your **$** correctly.

DON'T substitute any ideas. If you come up with another way to economize, add that concept to your day and figure it into the total.

DO calculate and record your savings as you achieve them. Trying to jog your memory isn't the most accurate way to arrive at your totals.

DO write your **$** on the detachable chart in pencil, so you can reuse the calendar should you wish to repeat the diet later in the year. (Money saving can be habit-forming.)

DO remember that some of the recommendations are based on a per person or product savings. You'll want to calculate your **$** for those suggestions by multiplying the initial savings by the number of people on the diet with you, or the number of any one product you need.

DON'T be concerned should you go off the diet for a few days. Just start where you left off.

DO make your daily savings visible by putting the cash in an envelope or jar. Looking at the currency piling up will be an added incentive to keep going.

DO enjoy following the plan, as you're really not being asked to make any sacrifices or to expend more energy than you normally do when shopping.

DO consider taking 15% of your total diet savings and treating yourself to a luxury. Then think about banking the rest for your future needs.

DO turn the page and start saving money while you're spending it.

WEEK ONE

Sunday—Day One

FOOD

Schedule a smorgasbord dinner with friends.
Kick off the diet with a mini-celebration by asking your friends to bring their best leftovers of
the week to your house. You'll enjoy a variety of
dishes and eliminate the need (*and* the expense)
of preparing tonight's meal.

A single's weekly food bill averages $29.22, the
daily cost $4.17; since 47¼% of an adult's nour-
ishment comes from dinner, the **$** is: $1.97

A couple's weekly food bill averages $53.57,
the daily cost $7.65; since they get 47¼% of their
nourishment from dinner, the **$** is: $3.62

A family of four's weekly food bill averages
$91.00, the daily cost $13.00; since they get 45%
of their nourishment from dinner, the **$** is: $5.85

(This suggestion, like so many others in the
diet, can be figured easily. Here you calculate
what dinner at home costs, and that's your **$**.)

TRANSPORTATION

Car owners: r **Don't warm up the engine, just
start and go.** Idling your motor for 90 seconds
uses the same amount of fuel that could take you
a distance of .75 mile if you were driving at 40
mph, so when you idle it wastes approximately
.04 gallon of gas (average cost of unleaded:
$1.391 per gallon). Turn on the ignition and try to
get moving immediately 18 times during the diet,
and you'll register a gasoline **$** of: $1.00

(Should you need assistance in figuring this $, see Calculation 1 in the Appendix)

CAUTION: Check your owner's manual first. Some engines must be warmed up or they will not run properly.

HOME MAINTENANCE

r Put two empty half-gallon milk cartons in the toilet tank. Cut off their tops, put them in the tank (positioned so they don't interfere with the flushing mechanism), and watch as they fill with water. Since the normal tank holds 6 gallons, it will now fill with only 5, and you'll save 4 gallons daily (based on going to the WC four times a day). Over 28 diet days that means 112 gallons conserved; water averages $1.00 per 1000 gallons, so the individual $ is 11.2¢ for a single's $ of: $0.11

A couple's $ of: $0.22

A family's $ of: $0.45

(In diet suggestions, such as this one, where we've given an individual $, we've carried it to the precision of one number after the decimal, and then rounded the figure out. This ensures accuracy. For example, here the individual $ is 11.2¢. A single would realize a $ of 11¢; a couple when that number is multiplied by 2, 22.4¢ or 22¢; a family of four, 44.8¢ or 45¢. As you can see, if the number beyond the decimal is 5 or more, we round the savings off to the next penny; if it's 4 or less, we keep the figure as is.)

PURCHASES

Snip facial tissues in half and double the quantity. How many times do you use a portion of a

18

tissue and then toss it out? By cutting the box in half, you'll not only have tissues that suit your needs, but you won't have to buy a 200-count two-ply box (79¢) as often. The per box **$**: $0.40

ENTERTAINMENT

Swap magazines with the smorgasborders. Encourage those who are coming tonight to bring their *read* periodicals so you can set up an exchange. (I recently traded *Us, Newsweek,* and *Country Living* for *McCall's, Cosmopolitan,* and *Cue/New York.*) Using the original cover price as a guide, the minimum **$** you could realize is: $1.25

Parents: Let the kids swap comic books—50¢ each—and add what they save into the total. Remember, you're all in this together!)

BONUS

Have clothing professionally repaired or rebuilt. Look through the closets to see if a pair of boots or shoes can be fixed, slacks narrowed, lapels restyled, or a jacket relined. Figure the cost of the alteration against purchasing a new piece of apparel and add the difference to the diet figures.

DAY 1 MINIMUM $: Singles, $4.73; Couples, $6.49; Families, $8.95

Monday—Day Two

FOOD

r Pack your lunch to avoid coffee shop and takeout-counter costs. It's an alternative to joining the "noonies," that eating cult who think brown-bagging it is a sin. Foolish worshippers, they—it's really a savings when you take: a chunk light tuna fish sandwich on wheat bread with lettuce and mayo (50¢); four chocolate chip cookies from a 19-ounce bag (13¢); a handful of potato chips from an 8-ounce package (13¢); soda from a six-pack (35¢); and an orange (18¢). The total cost is $1.29.

Compared to the coffee shop meal ($4.27), the per adult $ is $2.98, which *repeated each Monday on the diet means:* $11.92

Stacked against takeout-counter fare ($3.37), the per adult $ hits $2.08. *Done four times on the diet, it's:* $8.32 + *

(Moms and Dads: If you're making the children's lunch, but discover they can eat more cheaply and as nutritiously at the school cafeteria, let them. Then subtract your normal preparation costs from the Board of Education charges and add the $ to today's total.)

TRANSPORTATION

Car owners: r **Mark the speedometer with colored tape at two speeds.** Driving in town at 20 miles per hour (mph) instead of 30 reduces your miles per gallon (mpg) 13%. On the highway, cruising at 60 mph instead of 55 decreases your mpg by 5.6%. On 17 of the 28 days, you could conserve 2.72 gallons of gas (at $1.391 per gallon) by staying at 30 mph and 55 mph. That would mean a fuel $ of: $3.78 +

(See Calculation 2, Example 1)
Non-car owners: r **Purchase a monthly mass**

---

* This symbol used in calculating daily $.

transit pass. You could trim a minimum $2.00 off your commute with a pass, and probably cut the cost of weekend or evening travel expenses. Choose the appropriate schedule, and the per person $ is: $2.00

Or:

r Walk instead of taking mass transit. Avoiding public transportation (68¢ each ride) and walking saves money. Do it 24 times, perhaps either in the mornings or evenings as you go to or from work, and the per person $ is: $16.32

Or:

r Don't buy a mass transit transfer. By hoofing it the added distance 24 times while on the diet, you'll skip the extra ticket charge (33¢ each) and rack up a per person $ of: $7.92

Or:

r Go with a car pool, not on the commuter train. By being the fourth in a car (look for groups advertising on office and community bulletin boards) you really trim costs. The average daily round-trip commuter train ride is 49.76 miles ($\times$ 8¢ per mile = $3.98). Going the same distance in a car requires 2.9 gallons of gas ($\times$ $1.391 per gallon = $4.03); when that's shared by four, you pay $1.01. A 20-day car pool expense ($20.20) beats a 20-day commuter train pass ($79.60)—the per person $ is: $59.40

Both car and non-car owners: r Try supplementing these suggestions with "special hours" mass transit passes for schoolchildren, senior citizens, and the handicapped. Also, travel off-peak hours on commuter trains. Then factor whatever you glean into the 28-day total.

HOME MAINTENANCE

Depending on the season:

r Lower the thermostat 8 to 10 degrees, and reduce your annual heating bill 9% to 12%.

• On electric heaters, setting the dial back 8 degrees (going from 73°F/23°C to 65°F/18°C) can cut the yearly electric bill up to 10%. Since a consumer's total annual utility bill *averages* $459.16 (based on paying .0514¢ per kwh), the monthly **$** could be:$3.83

• With natural gas and oil heaters, moving back the setting 10 degrees (for example, from 72°F/22°C to 62°F/16°C) can mean a 9% to 12% yearly **$**.

Since the consumer's annual natural gas heating bill averages $394 (based on paying $3.43 per 1000 cubic feet), the monthly **$** might be:$3.45

Using the average yearly charge for oil heat, which is $710 (figured on oil costing 87¢ per gallon), the monthly **$** could be:$6.21

To accrue a **$** by lowering your thermostat, you really must take it down into the mid-60s or lower. Going from 80°F to 70°F won't give you as dramatic a **$**. Also, you'll want to remember that there are many factors affecting your heating costs beside the thermostat setting. For the best possible results, talk with your utility representative before you put this idea into effect.

Be careful if you're a senior citizen, or have a senior citizen or small children living with you. Both need a minimum indoor temperature of 65°F/18°C to avoid accidental hypothermia (lowering of the body temperature).

Or:

r Raise the air-conditioner dial from 72°F/ 22°C to 78°F/25°C and lower your cooling bill 39%.

A room air conditioner using 860 kwh from June to September costs $44.20 (.0514¢ per kwh) if you set it at 72°F; $27.12 at 78°F. That's a monthly $ of:

$4.27 +

A central air conditioner (30,000 BTUH, 2½- ton, with an EER [Energy Efficiency Rating] of 6) consuming 4750 kwh (.0514¢ per kwh) during the same four months can amount to $244.15 at 72°F; $149.79 at 78°F. Therefore, the monthly cooling $ is:

$23.59

(See Calculation 3)

If your air conditioner is like mine, it has no degree indicators, but is marked something like "low cool," "normal cool," and "super cool." There is also a knob that can be turned from 1 (warmer) to 5 (cooler). By putting a thermometer near the unit, you'll be able to figure which setting approximates 78°F.

PURCHASES

Shop the discount drugstore instead of the corner pharmacy. The neighborhood druggist has an 8.2-ounce tube of toothpaste ($2.67), a 16-ounce bottle of baby shampoo ($4.66), and a 10-ounce deodorant spray ($4.09). So does the discount store manager, but the prices for the same items run $1.64, $3.44, and $2.55, respectively. The benefit: a $ of:

$3.79

Increase your savings on the deodorant by switching from a spray to a stick, which gives you more uses for the money.

BONUS

Change telephone services. You could increase your total today if a call to the telephone business office indicates your *untimed service,* which most of us have, could be exchanged for *basic budget service* (for people with limited outgoing and incoming calls) or *timed service* (for those who don't indulge in lengthy conversations).

DAY 2 MINIMUM $: Singles, $20.16; Couples, $20.16; Families, $20.16

Tuesday—Day Three

FOOD

r Don't send out for coffee or tea. Make your own. One of the most subtle nickel-and-dime drains is the away-from-home cup of coffee or tea. You can combat this with BYOBTW (bring your own brew to work), which may mean you'll have to purchase a dime store 16-ounce thermos ($5.28) unless the office has a hot/cold water machine.

Over the next 19 workdays, drinking two cups daily from the takeout counter (at 37¢ per cup = $14.06) or a machine (at 20¢ = $7.60) costs more than making and taking it: coffee with cream and sugar (at 6¢ = $2.28) or tea with lemon and sugar (at 5¢ = $1.90). If you buy a thermos and prorate its cost over six months, that adds 1½¢ per cup, for a total of 57¢ over 19 days.

	Takeout	Machine
Coffee $ with thermos:	$11.21	$4.75 +
Coffee $ without thermos:	$11.78	$5.32
Tea $ with thermos:	$11.59	$5.13
Tea $ without thermos:	$12.16	$5.70

(You'll realize even more of a $ if you drink your stimulants straight.)

TRANSPORTATION

Car owners: r **Remove 100 pounds from your car.** Driving with 100 pounds of excess weight costs you .5 mpg. Why not remove unnecessary items from the trunk? Most people need little more than emergency tools, safety flares, and a spare tire. You could conserve 1.24 gallons of gas (at $1.391 per gallon) during the 16 workdays you'll be driving on the diet (two have passed; ten you'll be car-pooling with others). That could mean a fuel $ of:

$1.72

(See Calculation 2, Example 2)

HOME MAINTENANCE

r **Unplug your instant-on TV set.** It's drawing almost 20% of its power even when you have the knob on Off. Although you view the color set an average of 2200 hours annually, it's still consuming electricity those remaining 6560 hours that you're not watching. Stop using those unnecessary 314.88 kwh (at .0514¢ per kwh) every 12 months, or .86 kwh daily, and the 26-day $ is:

$1.15

(See Calculation 4)

25

PURCHASES

r Buy in bulk to avoid vending machines and candy counters. Packages of your favorite treats are available at discount drugstores and supermarkets: regular gum (ten for 95¢), sugarless gum (ten for $1.48), candy bars (six for $1.37), pop (six for $2.09), and cigarettes (ten packs for $6.21). Now compare your costs against theirs:

	Bulk	Vending Machine Candy Counter
Regular gum	10¢	29¢
Sugarless gum	15¢	29¢
Candy bars	23¢	33¢
Pop	35¢	47¢
Cigarettes	62¢	82¢

The minimum **$** for this idea, based on the candy bar six-pack: $0.60

BONUS

Buy seasonal fruits and vegetables. Select produce that's peaking, bruise-free, plump, firm, brightly colored, heavy for its weight, and fragrant. You could save up to 50% compared to the off-peak price while beating the cost of other fruits and vegetables that yet to hit (or have passed) their prime. Here's what's ready when:

FRUITS

Year-round: Avocados; Bananas; Lemons

January: Grapefruit; Oranges: Navel, Pineapple, Temple; Tangerines; Tangelos

February: Grapefruit; Oranges: Navel, Pineapple

March: Grapefruit; Oranges: Navel, Florida and Texas Valencia, Pineapple

April: Grapefruit; Oranges: Florida and Texas Valencia; Pineapple

May: Grapefruit; Oranges: Florida, Texas and Western Valencia; Pineapple

June: Apricots; Cherries; Grapes: California Perlette and Thompson seedless (usually expensive due to limited quantity); Limes; Melons; Cantaloupe; Watermelon; Oranges: Florida, Texas and Western Valencia; Peaches; Strawberries

July: Apricots; Blueberries; Cherries; Grapes: California Perlette and Thompson seedless (expensive due to limited quantity); Limes; Melons: Cantaloupe, Honeydew, Watermelon; Nectarines; Oranges: Western Valencia; Peaches; Plums

August: Blueberries; Grapes: Thompson seedless (less expensive variety), Cardinal Red, Queen varieties, Malaga; Melons: Cantaloupe, Casaba, Crenshaw, Honeydew, Persian, Watermelon; Nectarines; Oranges: Western Valencia; Peaches; Plums; Prunes

September: Apples: Red Delicious, MacIntosh, Golden Delicious, Jonathan; Grapes: Thompson seedless (less expensive variety), Cardinal Red, Queen varieties, Malaga, Concord; Melons: Casaba, Crenshaw, Honeydew, Persian; Oranges: Western Valencia; Peaches; Pears; Prunes

October: Apples: Red Delicious, MacIntosh, Stayman, Golden Delicious, Jonathan, Winesap; Coconuts; Cranberries; Grapes: Emperor (Red); Melons: Casaba, Honeydew; Oranges: Parson Brown, Hamlin; Pears; Prunes

November: Apples: Stayman, Winesap; Coconuts; Cranberries; Grapes: Emperor (Red); Oranges: Parson Brown, Hamlin; Pears; Tangelos

December: Coconuts; Cranberries; Oranges: Navel, Parson Brown, Hamlin, Pineapple; Tangerines; Tangelos

VEGETABLES

Year-round: Beets; Cabbage; Carrots; Celery; Greens; Lettuce; Mushrooms (skip August); Onions; Potatoes

January: Broccoli; Cauliflower; Chicory, Endive and Escarole; Sweet Potatoes; Turnips

February: Broccoli; Chicory, Endive and Escarole; Parsnips; Sweet Potatoes; Turnips

March: Broccoli; Chicory, Endive and Escarole; Peas; Parsnips; Sweet Potatoes

April: Artichokes; Asparagus; Broccoli; Chicory, Endive, and Escarole; Peas; Sweet Potatoes

May: Artichokes; Asparagus; Broccoli; Corn; Leeks; Peas; Radishes

June: Asparagus; Corn; Cucumbers; Green Beans; Leeks; Peas; Radishes; Tomatoes

July: Corn; Cucumbers; Green Beans; Leeks; Peppers: Green, Red; Radishes; Tomatoes

August: Corn; Cucumbers; Eggplant; Leeks; Peppers: Green, Red; Sweet Potatoes; Tomatoes

September: Cauliflower; Corn; Peppers: Green, Red; Sweet Potatoes

October: Broccoli; Brussels Sprouts; Cauliflower; Parsley; Pumpkins; Sweet Potatoes; Turnips

November: Broccoli; Brussels Sprouts; Cauliflower; Parsley; Pumpkins; Sweet Potatoes; Turnips

December: Broccoli; Brussels Sprouts; Cauliflower; Parsley; Sweet Potatoes; Turnips

I realize in many instances you'll see these fruits and vegetables in the stores earlier than the times I've listed. Those
are the first crops of the season and it's best to let them go.
The prices will come down shortly; then buy what you want.
In other cases, be sure they're not the first out of the field or
tree, which usually are not as tasty.

And don't overlook your regional produce, which could
peak earlier or later.

Finally, when most produce is in-season, especially in
June, frozen foods go on sale. It's a great time to stock your
freezer.

Figure your savings, each time you purchase, by compar-
ing what you pay for in-season items versus those that are
going "out."

*DAY 3 MINIMUM $: Singles, $8.22; Couples, $8.22;
Families, $8.22*

Wednesday—Day Four

FOOD

   **r Use cents-off coupons. Shop specials. Buy no-
name or store brands, *not nationally advertised
products*.** This is a great way to spend Wednes-
days (sometimes it's Thursdays or Fridays, depending on when the food pages highlight sales
in your daily newspaper). On a recent cruise
down my grocery store aisles, I could have saved:
25¢ with coupons (applesauce and salt); $1.00
buying a 3-pound-1-ounce box of no-name laundry detergent ($1.39) instead of the same-size
well-known national brand ($2.39); and $1.00 on
specials (100 tea bags for $1.69, not $2.39; a soda
pop six-pack at $1.99 instead of $2.29). My $:
$2.25 — 25¢ (for the extra daily newspaper I

bought to increase my coupon selection) = $2.00. You may exceed this, which I'm cutting in half so as not to stack the **$**: $1.00

The best way to use these three techniques is to shop the supermarket in your neighborhood that gives you the best buys each week, especially one that doubles or triples the worth of your coupons. Setting up a coupon exchange (see how-to books in your public library) is also helpful.

TRANSPORTATION

Car owners: **r Replace fouled spark plugs.** One misfiring plug can decrease your mpg 7%, and could cost you 2.07 gallons of gas (at $1.391 per gallon) during the next 15 diet driving days. Take the time to inspect the spark plugs at an auto shop or garage. For each one you buy ($1.11, but prorated over an average life of nine months: 12¢ and for 15 days: 6¢) at a discount store and install yourself, the fuel **$** is: $2.82

(See Calculation 2, Example 3)

HOME MAINTENANCE

r Substitute a sponge or dishcloth for paper towels. Handle spills with a sponge (27¢) or a cloth (you probably have one), and you may eliminate the need for a roll of paper towels (83¢) this month. The **$** is: $0.56

PURCHASES

r Dilute shampoo and double its use. You don't have to wash with shampoos at full strength. Clean your tresses with half the recommended

amount, diluting it with equal parts of water. The
$ per 16-ounce bottle ($3.44) is: $1.72

BONUS
   Sell something to a collector. "Found money"
is what most people call the experience of cashing
in on something they think is junk but a collector
considers gold: Barbie dolls, comic books, playing cards, china, etc. The value of most collect-
ibles is listed in directories in the public library. If
you score a sale, add those dollars to your total.

   DAY 4 MINIMUM $: Singles, $6.10; Couples,
$6.10; Families, $6.10

Thursday—Day Five

FOOD
   Trim meat costs with the butcher. You can turn
my pun into profit, because a butcher will show
you how to extend a beef buy beyond one meal.
He'll also tell you how to make less expensive
cuts tasty. For example, buy a seven-bone, 6-
pound pot roast about 2 to 2¼ inches thick ($1.83
per pound) rather than a comparable 6-pound-
14-ounce rib roast, bone-in (you need more meat
because of the bone), ($3.06 per pound) for a $
that's: $10.13

   The initial $ is just the beginning. Ask the
butcher to show you how to cut the pot roast into
three different meals. By removing the top blade
section, you have the most tender part ready for
panfrying: if you cut slices of meat about ½ inch
thick, it will yield two to three servings. Then

there's another section that can be cut into cubes and used for stew meat or soup or grind to create four servings. You can braise the final section as a pot roast, or chill and cut into thin strips to stir-fry, or into four thin steaks to marinate and broil. Whichever you choose, it'll yield four servings.

Cutting up beef like this really reduces your costs. Don't look at the initial price tag, but rather divide it by the number of servings you'll get. In this case, it's probably ten. Freeze what you can't eat in a few days.

TRANSPORTATION

Car owners: r **Inflate your tires to standard.** For every four pounds a tire is underinflated on your car the auto's mpg is decreased 2%. Test your tires' pressure when they're cold and, if necessary, bring them up to standard. (Refer to your owner's manual.) Over the next 14 driving days, that's .53 gallon of gas saved ($1.391 per gallon) for every four pounds you add per tire. The per tire fuel $ is: $0.73

(See Calculation 2, Example 4)

HOME MAINTENANCE

Make window cleaner; don't buy it. Since I've been mixing my own (¼ cup of ammonia to a quart of water: 6½¢) I've been avoiding the commercial 32-ounce window cleaner ($1.25), because the $ is: $1.19

If you don't have a spray bottle, ask a friend to give you any extra one.

PURCHASES

r **Turn used envelopes into memo pads.** Treasure the envelopes you receive in the mail, as each can be split open, then in half, and held together in a stack with a rubber band. The scraps make great telephone notes and shopping lists, and you don't have to buy a 60-sheet dime store pad (63¢). The **$** is: $0.63

BONUS

Shop sales. Each month is filled with promotions that can save you 20% to 50% on various items. Before you pay full price for something you need, check this list to see when it might go on special. Then add what you've saved to the diet total. (I've also indicated when holiday events are scheduled. At these times retailers can feature many different items, even those I've not specifically catalogued.)

January (also known as storewide clearance month): accessories; appliances; art supplies; baby needs; bicycles; blankets; books; china; costume jewelry; diamonds; dishes; drugs and cosmetics; floor coverings; foundations and lingerie; furs; glassware; handbags; housewares; luggage; men's and women's apparel; millinery; notions, yarns, and fabrics; shoes; stationery; stereos; television and radios; storm windows; toys; water heaters; white sales

February (time for final clearances, Valentine's Day, Lincoln and Washington Birthday sales): air conditioners; art supplies; bicycles; cars (used); fabrics; floor coverings and home furnishings; furs; hosiery; humidifiers; men's custom suits and general apparel; radios, televisions, and video cassette recorders; silverware; washers and dryers

March (pre-Easter sales mean spring fashion bargains): bedding; children's shoes; floor coverings; glassware; housewares; humidifiers; washers and dryers; winter sporting equipment

April: fabric; men's, women's, and children's fashion clearances; Mother's Day items; ranges

May (Memorial Day Weekend sales): baby needs; diamonds; dishwashers; home furnishings and housewares; house paints; luggage; microwave ovens; refrigerators; tires; white sales

June (graduation and Father's Day promotions): bathing suits; bedding; fabrics; floor coverings; foundations, lingerie, and sleepwear; freezers; frozen foods; home improvement items; hosiery; summer sportswear; televisions

July (Christmas in July events, Independence Day sales, and summer clearances): air conditioners; bedding; children's clothing; furniture (both indoor and out); handbags; millinery; fabric; summer sportswear; shoes; televisions and radios; white sales

August (final summer clearances, Labor Day sales, and general storewide clearances): accessories; air conditioners; baby needs; bedding; camping equipment; cars (new); draperies and curtains; fans; furniture; furs; gardening equipment; home-improvement items; housewares; lamps; school supplies and fashions; stationery; stereos; televisions; towels; washers and dryers

September (Labor Day sales continue, with home-improvement events): air conditioners; auto batteries; cars (new); china and glassware; coats; fabric; floor coverings; furniture

October (Columbus Day sales, furniture and home furnishings events): baby needs; bicycles; coats; china and glassware; fishing equipment and hunting needs; holiday entertainment items; hosiery; school supplies and fashions; toys

November (Christmas lay-away time begins; Election and Veterans Day, Thanksgiving and pre-Christmas sales): bicycles; blankets; cars (used); coats; furs; holiday entertainment items; men's and boy's suits; ranges; shoes; water heaters

December (clearance of holiday goods, post-Christmas sales, and post-Christmas card, gift wrap, ribbon sales): blankets;

children's apparel; coats; dishwashers; microwave ovens; shoes; televisions

DAY 5 MINIMUM $: Singles, $12.68; Couples, $12.68; Families, $12.68

Friday—Day Six

FOOD

r **Substitute nutritious treats for snacks.** Enjoy your munchies by switching from a 10-ounce box of pretzels (86¢) to a 1-pound bag of carrots (41¢); a 10-ounce bag of corn chips ($1.12) and ready-made dip (67¢) to a 9-ounce box of raisins ($1.31); and a 19-ounce package of chocolate chip cookies ($1.76) to a 4-pound bag of oranges ($1.38). By replacing your normal eats with those that have more substance, the $ is: $1.31

TRANSPORTATION

Car owners: r **Drive straight; don't weave.** Zipping from one lane to another while driving at 30 mph costs you 1.5 mpg. On the average round-trip journey to work (18.4 miles) you'll consume .56 gallon more gas daily ($1.391 per gallon) if you maneuver like Batman and Robin. Don't, and during the remaining 13 drive days you will get a fuel $ of: $10.13

(See Calculation 5)

HOME MAINTENANCE

r **Run a three-minute shower or a mini-tub.** On each Friday, Saturday, and Sunday during the diet, take a three-minute shower or a three-inch soak, and you'll consume approximately 21 gallons of water. That's opposed to 36 in a full tub. With the per person water consumption 45 gallons less each weekend, and 165 for the diet ($1.00 per 1000 gallons), the individual $ is 16.5¢ for a single's $ of: $0.17

A couple's $ of: $0.33

A family's $ of: $0.66

Showering or tubbing together—especially for children—can further reduce the water bill.

PURCHASES

Choose disposable razors, not refills. A package of five disposable razors ($1.19) beats the price of five refill blades ($2.28) for your razor. The $ is: $1.09

ENTERTAINMENT

Take in a cultural event on a local college campus. Music groups and other entertainers regularly tour colleges and universities, where the adult ticket ($7.57) is less expensive than one for a comparable big-name evening at the local arena ($14.00). That means a single's $ of: $6.43

A couple's $ of: $12.86

(Parents: Share baby-sitting responsibilities with friends or neighbors. What you don't spend can be added to your growing total.)

BONUS

Check utility bills to spot problems. Reviewing your electrical charges for the last 24 months could show you're using more kwh now. If you've added appliances, the increase may be warranted, but should the total seem high, call the company's business office. If you discover a malfunctioning thermostat appliance, such as a refrigerator, have it fixed, and boost the diet tally by what you'll save this month on kwh. Also, learn to read your meter to make sure the bill is accurate, and check whether you're entitled to any special rates. For example, if you have an electric water heater, some utility companies will charge you less per kwh.

DAY 6 MINIMUM $: Singles, $19.13; Couples, $25.72; Families, $26.05

Saturday—Day Seven

FOOD

Eat bacon ends instead of strips. Although the pieces may not look as pretty on the plate, 1 pound of bacon ends (79¢) is cheaper than strips ($1.67), and the **$** is: $0.88

TRANSPORTATION

Car owners: **Bypass road hazards or delays.** Rethink the way you drive to town, so your short trips of five miles or less are more fuel-efficient. By mapping a route that misses gravel or dirt roads and school zones, you won't travel at 20 mph, which can reduce your mpg by 13%. Instead you'll drive at 30 mph and realize a .1-gallon **$** ($1.391 per gallon) on each journey. The fuel **$** is: $0.14

(See Calculation 6)

HOME MAINTENANCE

Substitute community bulletin boards for the classifieds. Tacking a 3x5-inch card with your announcements ("Sofa for Sale"; "Jogging Partner

Wanted") on the supermarket, public library, laundry, club, and office bulletin boards (free) is a thrifty way to advertise. Since you won't need to pay for an ad in the weekly classifieds (15 words running for seven days: $4.00), the **$** is: $4.00

PURCHASES

Floss with thread. Topstitching thread (50 yards for 60¢) does the job of extra-fine unwaxed dental floss (50 yards for $1.50). The **$** is: $0.90

ENTERTAINMENT

Dial a long-distance friend for laughs. Calling a former flame, old pal, or family that has moved away is a nice way to have fun without spending a bundle (for example, at the movies). The rates all day today are 38% less than Sunday through Friday weeknights. On a 20-minute direct-dial call that spans the coasts, the charge is $3.76, not $6.11, for a **$** that's: $2.35

BONUS

Watch checkout clerks for mistakes. Let's face it, punching the cash register keys and dealing out change can lull even the most alert person into a coma. Your vigilance around dazed checkers and salespeople means money each time you spot a mischarged price or not enough cash returned to your palm. Whatever currency errors you catch throughout the diet should be applied to your total.

DAY 7 MINIMUM $: Singles, $8.27; Couples, $8.27; Families, $8.27

WEEK ONE MINIMUM **$**:   Singles, $79.29
Couples, $87.64
Families, $90.43

Congratulations! You've finished one week and I bet you're richer for it. Now onto the second.

WEEK TWO

Sunday—Day Eight

FOOD

Serve skim milk, not regular milk; ice milk instead of ice cream. A half gallon of skim milk (96¢) instead of the same amount of regular ($1.10) means a per half-gallon $ of: $0.14

And: selecting a half gallon of ice milk ($1.94) over as much ice cream ($2.24) is a per half-gallon $ of: $0.30

TRANSPORTATION

***Car owners:* Try lower-octane gasoline.** Your car may have less expensive tastes than you think. Try a lower octane, and if there's no knock as you accelerate, you've effectively started to lower fuel bills by switching from leaded premium ($1.45 per gallon) to a leaded regular ($1.24 per gallon). Based on an average gasoline tank holding 19.6 gallons, the $ is: $4.12

HOME MAINTENANCE

Snip a friend's plants and skip the dime store's. Cuttings from a neighbor's or friend's ivy and rhododendron are an inexpensive way to bring greenery into your life. (If you ask for growing instructions, you won't have to buy a book or make a trip to the public library.) Six tiny potted dime-store plants ($6.46) can't beat your $, based on a half dozen snips (free), a tray of six starter pots ($1.23), and a 4-pound bag of soil ($1.43): $3.80

PURCHASES
Use plastic bags instead of disposable gloves. Don't throw out plastic bags (free). They can double as disposable gloves (15¢ per pair) for dyeing hair, painting, and other odd jobs where you don't require heat-resistant protection. The per pair $ is: $0.15

ENTERTAINMENT
See what's free. The "Leisure" section of most Sunday newspapers lists movies, concerts, exhibits, sporting events, and other activities that have no admission charge. Go to one today rather than to a first-run movie where tickets average per adult ($4.25); per child ($2.36). That translates to a single's $ of: $4.25

A couple's $ of: $8.50

A family's $ of: $13.22

BONUS
Don't buy it. You know what I'm talking about. That certain something you cannot live without, *but deep down* know you can. Add the value of whatever you don't purchase to the total.

DAY 8 MINIMUM $: Singles, $12.76; Couples, $17.01; Families, $21.73

Monday—Day Nine

FOOD
Shop a thrift bakery. Your area's major bread manufacturer probably has outlets where day-old

bread is sold cheaper than the fresher stuff at the supermarket: a loaf of white (46¢ versus 74¢), rye (67¢, not 92¢), and wheat (61¢, as opposed to 81¢); a dozen dinner rolls (88¢ instead of $1.34). Purchasing three loaves of bread and two packages of rolls is a **$** of:

$1.65

(Freeze what you can't eat.)

TRANSPORTATION

Car owners: **Buy oil at the discount store, not the gas station.** A quart can of 10/30W or 10/40W oil at the discount store ($1.09) on an average is less than at the gas station ($1.78), so the **$** is:

$0.69

HOME MAINTENANCE

Cash in aluminum cans. You're not cleaning up, monetarily speaking, if you're throwing out aluminum cans. Each pound (23 cans) dropped off at a recycling center (you may be surprised how close one is to your home or the shopping mall) could mean 26¢. Start hoarding now, and supplement the pile by asking neighbors for their discards. Figure the minimum **$** based on a 2-pound salvage:

$0.52

The easiest way to locate a recycling center is to contact an environmental group listed in the Yellow Pages under "Environmental, Conservation & Ecological Organizations."

PURCHASES

Report misdialed local calls for credit. Connecting with the wrong person can be embarrassing and costly, as it's a message unit (6¢). By telling the credit operator of your mistake, the charge is erased from your phone bill. Since most of us hit an incorrect digit at least once a month, the minimum $ is: $0.06

BONUS

Get throwaways before the sanitation crew. Becoming a scavenger has its advantages. (I rescued an old townhouse fireplace mantelpiece, which has been appraised at $100, from the trash and—please note, ***non-car owners***—carried it three blocks to work.) By checking when the refuse collection is scheduled in your vicinity, you can search the streets before the truck. Then figure the worth of what you find and add its value to the total.

DAY 9 MINIMUM $: Singles, $2.92; Couples, $2.92; Families, $2.92

Tuesday—Day Ten

FOOD

Select regional and seasonal fish as opposed to "out-of-towners." The fish market's owner can tell you the best local buys (sea trout, mackerel, cod, monk, catfish, whitefish, Pacific red snapper) which average $2.30 per pound. That's better than the more popular species, flounder, sole, and swordfish, which he has shipped in at $5.26 per pound. Based on two to three servings per pound, the individual serving $ is $1.184 for a single's $ of: $1.18

A couple's $ of: $2.37

A family's $ of: $4.74

TRANSPORTATION

Car owners: **Let rain wash the auto.** Be happy
when it pours. That's how a friend of mine cleans
his car. When the storm stops he wipes the vehicle dry with a cloth and then polishes it with a
chamois, thereby avoiding the need for a professional wash ($3.30). The **$** is: $3.30

HOME MAINTENANCE

Handle multiple light needs with one bulb. In
those fixtures where you have two lights, for example two 75-watt bulbs, remove them. Put a
100-watter in one socket, a burned-out bulb in
the other. If you use the light 30 minutes daily for
the next 19 diet days, you'll consume .95 kwh, not
1.43 kwh (.0514¢ per kwh), and the **$** could be: $0.02

When figuring any of the kwh **$**, just follow
these two steps:

1. $\dfrac{\text{watts saved} \times \text{hours used daily}}{1000}$ = kwh savings

2. Kwh saved daily × your kwh cost × number of
   days applied = **$**

PURCHASES

Wear two pantyhose, each with a good leg.
Save your pantyhose if only one leg is run, snip-
ping the bad "gam" off at the thigh. Then slip the
one-legged pair on with another snagged pair of
the same color whose opposite bad leg has also
been removed. For each department store pair
($2.92) you don't purchase, the **$** is: $2.92

For every dime-store pantyhose ($1.57) you
won't need, the **$** is: $1.57**+**

Not only does this idea save you money, but by wearing two pantyhose your tummy receives extra support.

And/or:

Stock two pairs of the same color socks. Then when one gets lost or holey, you're not left without a mate (would that relationships were as easy to mend). Extending a set this way lets you avoid buying a new pair of department store dress or casual socks ($2.64), for a $ of: $2.64

Or a dime-store version ($1.42) for a $ that's: $1.42 +

BONUS

Buy slightly damaged goods. If you find a shirt missing a few buttons, a soap box or a cereal box that's been slit but whose contents haven't been harmed, or a briefcase with a minute gouge, ask for its price to be reduced. Using this idea throughout the diet could increase your total frequently, so keep tabs on what you accumulate.

DAY 10 MINIMUM $: Singles, $7.49; Couples, $8.68; Families, $11.05

Wednesday—Day Eleven

FOOD

Cut food costs. Don't shop on an empty stomach. Pushing your cart down the supermarket aisles when you're hungry can increase the checkout counter receipt 10% to 15%. Eat a little before you shop, and singles spending $29.22 weekly will have a $ of: $3.65

A couple shelling out $53.57 each week produces a $ of: $6.70

A family whose costs hit $91.00 weekly at the grocery store can see a $ of: $11.38

(Moms and Dads: If you usually take your children to market, don't. Each can add $1.00 to the food bill, so tabulate what you save this week by asking a friend to watch your kids, and add that figure to your total.)

TRANSPORTATION

Car owners: **Carpet swatches make good car mats.** Picking up 18x27-inch carpet samples at a floor-covering outlet ($2.00 each)·is a smart buy over the same size car mats at an auto supply store ($9.00 each). Choose two colorful swatches for beneath the front seats, spray them with a 16-ounce can of fabric protector ($4.07) to help resist soil and stains (½ can for each sample), and you've a $ that's: $9.93

HOME MAINTENANCE

Stop a leaky faucet. A dripping tap can mean a loss of 15 gallons of water daily, or 270 gallons ($1.00 per 1000 gallons) in the next 18 days. By fixing the leak yourself (there are books at the public library) with a washer (5¢), the per faucet $ is: $0.22

PURCHASES

Visit a beauty school instead of a salon. Beauty and barber schools' haircuts ($3.90), wash and sets or blow-drys ($3.33), and manicures ($2.06) outdo salon and shop prices ($8.14, $8.67, and

$6.33, respectively). Watch to see which student is best at styling while *you* enjoy a manicure and a **$** of: $4.27

BONUS
   Take advantage of a friend's "trading up." You probably know someone who *must* always have the latest, be it a stereo, tape recorder, or camera. By taking advantage of his or her consumer mania, you could buy a slightly used product quite reasonably. Do consider its previous use and current warranty before you purchase. Whatever you save adds nicely to your total.

   DAY 11 MINIMUM $: Singles, $18.07; Couples, $21.12; Families, $25.80

Thursday—Day Twelve

FOOD
   Choose pet food by ingredients rather than by brand name. Lowering a cat's or dog's feeding costs is easy once you know what to look for on the label. The words to spot are "complete," "balanced," or "contains all the ingredients necessary as established by the National Academy of Sciences (NAS) or National Research Council (NRC)." Those phrases indicate your animal is getting the proper nutrients, even if the price is low and the label's name is unknown. In fact, here's how it stacks up:

Lesser-known Brands	*Name Brands*
Dogs	
26¢ (14-ounce can)	43¢ (14-ounce can)
$1.55 (5-pound bag)	$2.37 (5-pound bag)

Cats

42¢ (12-ounce can)   36¢ (6½-ounce can)
91¢ (12-ounce box)   94¢ (12-ounce box)

So dog lovers who buy ten cans and one bag of dry food could total up a $ that's: $2.52

Cat fanciers, purchasing four 12-ounce cans and two boxes of dry food, could realize a $ of: $1.26+

TRANSPORTATION

Car owners: r **Leave the car where it'll spend the night.** Having to move the auto from the curb or the driveway into the garage (100 feet) consumes between 1¢ and 2¢ of gasoline, but the drive can add as much engine wear to the car as a 500-mile trip, so the hidden maintenance costs could be severe. You see, most engine wear occurs during starting the car and the first ten seconds of operation. Repeat this tip six times during the diet, and the $ is: $0.06

HOME MAINTENANCE

Don't replace the ironing board cover; repair it. Ironing board covers are like bodies: The first thing to go is the middle. If only stomachs could be put into shape this easily! Iron-on patches (two, 5x7-inch: 95¢) can be put over the holes and help you delay buying a new cover ($3.99), for a $ of: $3.04

PURCHASES

Make a baking soda and water mouthwash. I find that in the morning a teaspoon of baking soda and a half glass of water rivals a 1-ounce swig from an 18-ounce bottle of brand-name breath freshener ($1.82). My 16-ounce box of baking soda (44¢) gives me 96 uses (½¢ each); the bottle only 18 washes. The per 16-ounce box **$** is: $9.27

Figure it this way:

$$\frac{\text{your mouthwash cost}}{\text{no. washes in bottle}} \times \begin{array}{c}\text{no. of washes}\\ \text{in your}\\ \text{baking soda}\end{array} - \begin{array}{c}\text{your}\\ \text{baking soda}\\ \text{costs}\end{array} = \text{\$}$$

BONUS

Share an item's cost to reduce your investment. Ask friends or neighbors to participate in the cost and use of an appliance such as a food processor or piece of equipment like a power lawn mower. Then apply the dollars you don't lay out to your total.

DAY 12 MINIMUM $: Singles, $13.63; Couples, $13.63; Families, $13.63

Friday—Day Thirteen

Don't let the day and number spook you. There are too many lucky money-saving ideas to carry out.

FOOD

Pass over veal cutlets for turkey cutlets. Tonight why not prepare piccatta made with turkey cutlets ($2.27 per pound) rather than veal ($6.94 per pound). Since you'll receive three servings to a pound for either cut, the individual serving **$** is $1.556, for a single's **$** of: $1.56

A couple's **$** of: $3.11

A family's **$** of: $6.22

Consider working two butchers before carrying through this tip. That way you can play the "prodigal shopper" by returning to one only when your budget can't do better by the other. Why not select a supermarket butcher and one that has an independent store?

TRANSPORTATION

Car owners: **Eliminate a five-mile drive.** Delay an errand until tomorrow (procrastination can pay off). By avoiding a short drive today, you won't squander .64 gallon of gas ($1.391 per gallon) and the fuel $ will be: $0.89

You can compute it like this:

$$1. \quad \frac{5}{\text{your mpg at 30mph}} = \frac{\text{your gallon}}{\text{savings per}} \atop \text{five-mile trip}$$

2. Gallons savings per five miles $\times$ your gas cost per gallon = **$**

HOME MAINTENANCE

Cut steel wool soap pads in half. Normally you use only a section of a scouring pad before you set it aside on the sink to dry. Unfortunately, that's when it usually starts rusting and leaving a mess. By cutting each new pad in half, you'll extend the life of an 18-pad box ($1.07) twice as long and keep your counters cleaner. The per box $ is: $0.54

Be sure to cut each pad over the sink. That way you can wash away the soap powder that tends to sprinkle out as you snip through the steel wool.

PURCHASES

Make a dog bone. Sterilize a marrow or knucklebone (the butcher should have one if you don't) for 30 minutes in boiling water and you've a gift for your pet or a friend's. The bone (free) is less than a commercial one ($1.40), so the $ is: $1.40

ENTERTAINMENT

Shop paperback exchanges for discounted softcovers. A paperback exchange lets you sell your softcovers (based on the original price) for a 15% *credit*. That "money" can be applied against a used paperback, often sold at 50% of its initial cost. Recently I received an 87¢ credit on a spy thriller and ended up paying only 88¢ for that week's third most popular U.S. paperback. (New, it would have been $3.50.) Since most softcovers are averaging $3.40, the per book $, even without a credit, is: $1.70

BONUS

Trade clothing with friends. Swapping apparel that no longer fits helps fill in a wardrobe. Whatever you realize from the exchange, be sure to add its worth to the diet total.

DAY 13 MINIMUM $: Singles, $6.09; Couples, $7.64; Families, $10.75

Saturday—Day Fourteen

FOOD

Substitute chunk light tuna for solid pack; and margarine sticks for tubs, squeeze bottles, and butter.

1. Serve chunk light tuna (6½-ounce can: $1.04) rather than solid pack (6½-ounce can: $1.34), for a per can $ of: $0.30

And:

2. Use a 1-pound box (four sticks) of store brand margarine (57¢) instead of: a 1-pound box of a nationally advertised brand (81¢) and the $ is: $0.24 +

Or:

A 1-pound tub of name brand margarine (89¢), which means a $ that's: $0.32

Or:

A 1-pound squeeze bottle of well-known margarine (96¢) for a $ of: $0.39

Or:

A 1-pound box (four sticks) of name brand butter ($2.02) and a $ that registers: $1.45

TRANSPORTATION

Car owners: **Don't keep the engine running when you're out of the car.** Few of us are track stars, yet we've all been known to leave the motor on while we dash for a newspaper or a pay telephone booth. Instead of idling your car 2 minutes, turn off the engine and then restart the car (takes as much gas as a ½ minute of idling) when you're ready to go. You'll save 1½ minutes of idling time, which burns up .04 gallon of gas ($1.391 per gallon), and the fuel $ could be: $0.06

(See Calculation 1)

HOME MAINTENANCE

Trade services with a friend. A neighbor or pal probably does something better than you around the home, and you may be great at another chore. By swapping services (washing windows; altering clothes; upholstering furniture; polishing silver; painting the kitchen), you can reduce labor expenses. Figure the $ based on what a professional would charge, or two hours at minimum wage ($3.35 per hour) for a $ of: $6.70

PURCHASES

Arrange tree branches rather than flowers. Picked from your yard (free) or purchased at the florist ($2.00), tree branches (lemon, magnolia) are less expensive than a flower shop's ready-made bouquet ($2.44). They also give a thrifty decoration for tonight's festivities, because the $ is: $0.44

ENTERTAINMENT

Invite guests who will bring food. Do yourself a favor and ask four to five friends to bring food for this evening's dinner party: hors d'oeuvres (sharp cheddar cheese and crackers: $3.72); wine (1.5 liters: $4.08); salad (tossed green with carrots and celery plus French dressing: $1.63); dinner rolls ($1.34); a side dish (asparagus: $1.05); and dessert (frozen layer-cake: $2.64). With you preparing the entree, coffee, and tea, the $ is: $14.46

I know what you're thinking, but no, I'm not a heartless hostess. I began to use this technique only because I couldn't cook. When I asked people for dinner, they'd automatically offer to bring the entrees, vegetable, or dessert; I guess they figured that would cost them less than a stomach pump.

What I soon discovered was everyone got involved, and each tried to outdo the others in the delicacies they brought. As a result, I'm now known for my tasty and entertaining parties.

BONUS

Reduce credit card balance to $0.00. Pay off at least one charge account this month so you won't have to see some of your money go for interest. Whatever you save, factor into your total.

DAY 14 MINIMUM $: Singles, $22.20; Couples, $22.20; Families, $22.20

WEEK TWO MINIMUM $:   Singles, $83.16
Couples, $93.20
Families, $108.08

You're at the midway point in *The Money Diet*. If your totals are matching or exceeding the minimums, that's great. Should you be a little behind, don't worry. Here come the final two weeks, and there are a lot of ideas to increase your savings.

WEEK THREE

Sunday—Day Fifteen

FOOD

Families: **Picnic at home.** Put a blanket on the floor and tell stories while devouring all-meat hot dogs, marshmallows, potato chips, fruit, and soda ($6.46). That's instead of today's fast food hamburger stop ($9.10) for a $ of: $2.64

Singles and couples: Picnic, too, but why not serve wine, chicken, salad, and fruit for two ($10.40) on the floor. (You can tell stories or use your romantic imagination.) For not having dinner at a restaurant ($29.20 for two), the single's **$** is: $9.40

The couple's **$** is: $18.80

TRANSPORTATION

Car owners: **Skip the Sunday drive.** It can be a 30-mile round trip to nowhere, providing traffic-jammed aggravation and backseat frustration. Don't take the ride, and conserve 1.75 gallons of gas ($1.391 per gallon) for a fuel **$** of: $2.43

Arrive at your **$** this way:

1. $\dfrac{\text{your Sunday drive miles}}{\text{your mpg at 55 mph}} = \begin{array}{l}\text{your gallons}\\\text{saved per}\\\text{Sunday drive}\end{array}$

2. Gallons saved per Sunday drive × your gas cost per gallon = **$**

HOME MAINTENANCE

r Run the tap only when necessary. You can save 1 gallon of water by filling the basin when washing hands, 2 to 4 by doing the same when shaving, and almost 2 as you brush your teeth (wet the brush and use a glass of water to rinse). Following these tips, you'll conserve an average of 6 gallons daily, 84 in the next 14 days ($1.00 per 1000 gallons). That means an individual **$** of 8.4¢ for a single's **$** of: $0.08

The couple's **$** is: $0.17

A family's **$** is: $0.34

PURCHASE

Squeeze a tube with a can key. Why buy a special adapter (88¢) to push out more toothpaste? Look in your kitchen drawers for a metal key (free), the type that's attached to canned meat tins. Put that key at the base of the tube and wind it toward the top each time you brush. I'm not calculating the additional cleanings you'll achieve with this device, but since you don't have to purchase an adapter, the **$** is: $0.88

ENTERTAINMENT

Follow your newspaper's television directory, not the newsstand's. Do you really need a special weekly TV magazine (50¢)? Refer to the one in the Sunday paper (free) and the **$** is: $0.50

BONUS

Scan the classified ads before paying top dollar. If you spot what you need and find the quality right, purchase it. Then add what you've saved to the monthly total.

DAY 15 MINIMUM $: Singles, $13.29; Couples, $22.78; Families, $6.79

Monday—Day Sixteen

FOOD

Eat beef rather than calves' liver. For a change, serve beef liver ($1.17 per pound) instead of calves' liver ($2.83 per pound). Based on four servings per pound, the individual serving **$** is 41.5¢ for a single's **$** of: $0.42

A couple's **$** of: $0.83

A family's **$** of: $1.66

TRANSPORTATION

Car owners: r **Car-pool for the next two weeks.**
Joining three others in an auto for the average
18.4-mile round trip to work means you're shar-
ing the daily cost of 1.07 gallons of gas ($1.391
per gallon). Since you usually absorb the total
expense ($1.49), it should feel good to have to
pay only 37¢. Keep it up for the next ten workdays, and the fuel $ comes in at: $11.20

HOME MAINTENANCE

**Let mothballs deodorize/repel insects in gar-
bage.** Four mothballs (94 in a 1-pound box:
$1.57) tossed into an indoor kitchen and outdoor
garbage can, twice a week for the next two weeks,
eliminates the need for using between five and six
ounces of a 16-ounce ant and roach spray ($2.44)
and two self-adhesive deodorants (54¢ each), for
a $ that's: $1.41

PURCHASES

Dry clean by the pound, not the garment. Taking clothes that don't need special attention to the
coin dry cleaner's (8 pounds = 6 to 7 pieces:
$4.63) gets more for your money than piecemeal
dry cleaning: two sweaters ($4.50); one wool
dress ($4.26) *or* one pair of slacks ($2.40); a vest
($1.63); and two blazers ($5.25). The difference in
prices means a $ (based on one pair of slacks)
that's: $9.15+

Or (based on the wool dress): $11.01

BONUS

Cancel a credit card policy if you're covered.
Review your home insurance to see if you're pro-

tected for loss and robbery outside the house or apartment. If you are, cancel any special credit card insurance, and add the premium payments you don't make to your total.

DAY 16 MINIMUM $: Singles, $22.18; Couples, $22.59; Families, $23.42

Tuesday—Day Seventeen

FOOD

Revive stale bread. Tossing out bread is wasteful. Why not sprinkle water on the hard slices and then toast? They'll be eatable, and you may find that by bringing a minimum of four slices "back" from a 16-ounce loaf, the **$** for supermarket white bread (74¢ a loaf) will be: $0.16

The **$** for a similar thrift bakery package (46¢ a loaf) could be: $0.10+

HOME MAINTENANCE

r Turn off the lights that are not in use. How often do you sit in one room while a bulb burns needlessly in another part of the house? During the remaining diet days, switch off any light as you leave the room. Based on using a 100-watt bulb seven hours less during the diet (.70 kwh at .0514¢ per kwh), the **$** is: $0.04

I'm using the 100-watt example to represent a series of bulbs, you'll probably be flipping off. And for those who think frequent turning on and off of lights shortens a bulb's life, here's a nice surprise: There's a net **$** when you switch off an incandescent light for more than 3 minutes, a fluorescent lamp for more than 15 minutes.

PURCHASES

Get scrap paper at the printer's. Hundreds of sheets of paper are tossed out by print shops. Have the scraps discarded instead into a box you provide. Mine filled with 500 sheets in one day. The charge: $0.00. True, some of the paper had writing on one side, but even if you halve the cost of the cheapest paper you can buy, foolscap (500 sheets: $2.95), the **$** is: $1.48

BONUS

Go for free financial help. The Consumer Credit Counseling Service (there are about 200 nationwide) is a public service that will mail you a do-it-yourself budget sheet (free) with money-saving techniques. The office staff can also answer questions. Consider what you'd pay a similar consultant, and increase your total by that number.

DAY 17 MINIMUM $: Singles, $1.62; Couples, $1.62; Families, $1.62

Wednesday—Day Eighteen

FOOD

Serve lamb blade or round bone chops, not loin chops. Lamb needn't be out of your dollar reach, if you purchase chops from the shoulder ($3.00 per pound) instead of from the loin ($4.05 per pound). Based on two servings per pound, the individual serving **$** is 52.5¢ for a single's **$** of: $0.53

   A couple's **$** of: $1.05

   A family's **$** of: $2.10

HOME MAINTENANCE

r Find the phone number yourself. By not calling "information," which usually starts charging after the first six requests (18¢), you can stop paying extra for numbers your fingers can find in the White or Yellow Pages. In some cities, if you don't use up your "free" calls to information they become credits (10¢) applied against your bill. Don't let anyone dial the information operator, even guests, throughout the diet days and the **$** could be: $0.18

PURCHASES

Try a disposable pen and forget the refill. Writing with a pen you can toss out (29¢) when it's dry can be as satisfying as putting a refill ($1.09) in your ballpoint shell. The added pleasure is a **$** of: $0.80

BONUS

Rethink food portions. A University of Arizona study found that in two U.S. cities, families were tossing out 15% of the food they bought. Review what you've put in the garbage and consider whether you're buying too much. Perhaps you don't need that extra half pound of meat or gallon of milk. (The U.S. Department of Agriculture's booklet *Family Food Budgeting*, Home and Garden Bulletin #94, which singles and couples can use as well, offers suggestions on selecting proper nutritional food portions.) Should you be able to reduce the amount of groceries you lug home, figure your dollar savings and add it to the total.

DAY 18 MINIMUM $: Singles, $1.51; Couples, $2.03; Families, $3.08

Thursday—Day Nineteen

FOOD

Make your own breaded fish sticks. Frozen fillets ($2.58 per pound) you buy and bread crumbs you make (19¢) are less expensive than the already breaded fish ($3.03 per pound). Considering there are usually three servings to a pound, the individual serving $ is 8.8¢ for a single's $ of: $0.09

A couple's $ of: $0.18

A family's $ of: $0.35

HOME MAINTENANCE

Deodorize with baking soda. A refrigerator can handle its smells with a 16-ounce box of baking soda (44¢), so you won't need a self-adhesive deodorant (54¢). The $ is: $0.10

PURCHASES

Give a frame as a gift. It's usually impossible to go through a month without having to buy a present. Why not choose a 5x7-inch decorator frame ($8.00), which everyone can use and is less than the average gift ($10.00) we often end up giving. The $ is: $2.00

BONUS

Shop factory outlets. Items ranging from apparel to home furnishings are sold in factory outlets at prices near wholesale. (I've saved quite a bit casing these places—most recently, $8.00 on a pair of leather moccasins.) If you find you've economized by going to one of these stores, add the dividends to your total.

DAY 19 MINIMUM $: Singles, $2.19; Couples, $2.28; Families, $2.45

Friday—Day Twenty

FOOD

Pick sugarless and non-individually packed cereals. A 12-ounce box of sugar-free cornflakes (94¢) is a better buy than a 15-ounce box of sugar-coated flakes ($1.47) because the $ is: $0.24

And:

A 1-pound-2-ounce box of oatmeal (88¢) gives you more for your money than individually wrapped servings in a 10-ounce package ($1.17), which makes the $, based on an 18-ounce box: $1.23

Take advantage of your supermarket's unit pricing label under each of these products, so you can figure the per pound $. Then multiply that number by the size of what I recommend you buy. That's your $.

HOME MAINTENANCE

Use a measuring cup. Putting in the exact amount saves money. When I began to carefully pour 1¼ cups into the washer, as opposed to 2, I started getting 15 washes from my 3-pound-1-ounce no-name brand detergent ($1.44), not 9. That turned out to be a $ of: $0.96

(See Calculation 7)

PURCHASES

Treasure food containers from supermarket buys. Food is now packaged in wonderful reusable plastic bowls and bottles. For each 4-cup plastic container bowl ($1.76) you don't buy in the dime store, the $ is: $1.76

For every 1-quart plastic juice bottle ($1.16) you needn't purchase, the $ is: $1.16 +

(Parents: Many of these containers make great tub toys. Should you be able to substitute any of them for a rubber duck or boat, add the savings into the total.)

ENTERTAINMENT

Eat breakfast out, not dinner. Plan to enjoy a meal away from home this weekend, but make it in the A.M., when the spread—two adults ($11.00) and two children ($4.00)—is cheaper than in the P.M.: two adults ($19.80) and two kids ($7.20). The occasion can be as delicious, and for singles the $ is: $4.84

For couples the $ is: $8.80

For families the $ is: $12.00

BONUS

Barter for goods or services. You can get something without exchanging money by bartering, from having a room painted to acquiring a bicycle. The organizations are listed in the Yellow Pages under "Barter" or "Trading." (Check with your Better Business Bureau branch for a group's credentials before you get involved.) When you connect with a trade, factor its dollar value into the total. (If the item or service you receive in the exchange is worth more than $100, be sure to discuss it with your accountant or the Internal Revenue Service, as it can be considered income.)

DAY 20 MINIMUM $: Singles, $8.43; Couples, $12.39; Families, $15.59

Saturday—Day Twenty-One

FOOD

Buy sugar and flour by the bag and in bulk, rather than by the box or can. A 5-pound box of white flour ($1.19, at 24¢ per pound) versus a 13.5-ounce can (52¢, at 62¢ per pound) means that by purchasing the 5-pound bag the $ is: $1.89

And:

A 5-pound bag of granulated white sugar ($1.88, at 38¢ per pound) instead of a 2-pound box (92¢, at 46¢ per pound) translates to a per bag $ of: $0.42

Here's another example where unit pricing labels will assist your calculations. Don't forget to multiply the per pound savings by the size of the product I recommend you purchase.

TRANSPORTATION

***Car owners:* Call ahead for what you need.** By using the phone and not the car you might be able to eliminate an unnecessary five-mile trip.

That means you'll conserve .64 gallon of gas ($1.391 per gallon) for a $ of: $0.89+

Non-car owners: **Do the same** and save a fare (68¢ each way) for a $ that's: $0.68

HOME MAINTENANCE

Replace 100-watt bulbs with 50-watt reflectors. Pole and other bell-shaped lamps are often more efficient and effective with 50-watt reflector bulbs ($4.75 each). Although they cost more than 100-watters (75¢ each), they use half the electricity while giving a more directed beam of light. Don't look at the price tag of the reflectors, but at the manufacturer's projected electricity savings over the life of the light ($5.00, based on 5¢ per kwh). That means the per bulb $ is: $1.00

We found the $ by:

1. Kwh savings — cost of the 50 watt reflector = lifetime savings on the bulb
2. Cost of the 100-watt bulb you didn't buy + lifetime savings on the 50-watt reflector bulb = $

PURCHASES

Freeze water into a block of ice. A used half-gallon milk carton filled with water ($1.00 per 1000 gallons: .05¢) put in the freezer eventually makes a perfect "coolant" for an ice chest. Compared to a 5-pound bag of ice (49¢), the $ is: $0.49

ENTERTAINMENT

Use the public library's books and records. The practice can trim your leisure budget $10.00 for every hardcover, $5.00 for each children's book, and $6.00 per record. One trip could mean a minimum $ of: $10.00

Figure your $ based on each record's and book's cover price, listed on the dust jacket or as part of the library's filing code.

BONUS

Visit a charity thrift shop for bargains. These secondhand stores have great apparel, housewares, and home furnishings fill-ins. Frames, silverware, T-shirts, mixing bowls, cooking tins, scarves, and so forth are often marked at bargain prices. Keep track of how you reduce your expenses, and put those numbers into the total.

DAY 21 MINIMUM $: Singles, $14.69; Couples, $14.69; Families, $14.69

WEEK THREE MINIMUM $:   Singles, $63.91
Couples, $78.38
Families, $67.64

That's three weeks down and one to go. Just seven more days before you tabulate your grand total.

Good luck, and keep saving.

WEEK FOUR

Sunday—Day Twenty-two

FOOD

Take your refreshments to the movies. By making your own treats you'll find the size you eat less fattening, and you won't get a hernia carrying one of those gigantic boxes, cups, or candy bars to your seat. Here's how the costs stack up:

		Yours	Theirs	
Popcorn	64¢	(10-ounce can)	$1.25	(medium box)
Candy bar	45¢	(two eat for the price of one when you compare sizes)	78¢	
Soda	35¢		84¢	

Since most of us go for popcorn, the minimum **$** is: $0.61

TRANSPORTATION
Car owners: **Pump your own gas.** We found self-service gasoline stations charged an average of 14¢ less per gallon for premium and unleaded fuel than where attendants fill the tank. Pump an average 19.6-gallon tank three-quarters full, and the **$** is: $2.06

HOME MAINTENANCE
Use hand towels for bathtub window curtains. Hand towels ($2.60 each) can provide privacy and a decorative touch to the bathroom, as they're just the right size for most tub windows. If you're not Betsy Ross, have a friend show you how to whipstitch two towels so they slip onto a rod. Compared to 30x24-inch ready-made curtains ($10.99) that fill the same area, the **$** is: $5.79

PURCHASES
Put baking soda in your footwear instead of odor-killing insoles. A 16-ounce box of baking

soda (44¢) can keep boots, sneakers, and street shoes as fresh-smelling as those special insoles ($2.25). By sprinkling the baking soda into your footwear, letting them stand overnight, and then shaking them clean in the morning, you can handle most odors. For every pair of insoles you don't have to buy, the **$** is: $1.81

ENTERTAINMENT

See a second-run film. Catch a movie at a theater that shows pictures several months after they've been released. The per adult admission ($2.46) and per child ticket ($1.21) are less than a premiere house's (per adult: $4.25; per child: $2.36). That means the single's **$** is: $1.79

The couple's **$** is: $3.58

The family's **$** is: $5.88

BONUS

Shop with a friend's employee discount. Ask someone you know who might have an employee discount if it's OK for you to use it. (Of course, you'll want to offer a favor in return.) Calculate the **$** on every item you purchase, and add it to the diet total.

DAY 22 MINIMUM $: Singles, $12.06; Couples, $13.85; Families, $16.15

Monday—Day Twenty-three

FOOD

Purchase bulk, mild, and domestic cheese. If you love cheese, buy mild cheddar in a bulk

package ($2.51 per pound), not sharp cheddar in
bulk ($2.73 per pound), for a per pound $ of: $0.22 +

Or:
Buy a domestic cheese ($2.05 per pound)
rather than an imported Brie ($5.63 per pound),
for per pound $ of: $3.58

Or:
Select a mild cheddar in a bulk package ($2.51
per pound), not grated in a package ($2.93 per
pound), for per pound $ of: $0.42

TRANSPORTATION

Car owners: How's car pooling?

Non-car owners: You're coming into the
stretch, you walking, mass-transit-passing, and
car-pooling people. Keep it up.

HOME MAINTENANCE

Dial 800 and receive free information. If you
call 1-800-555-1212, a telephone operator will let
you know if a company has a special complaint
or information hotline. If the corporation doesn't,
touch base with its branch office in your region
and ask that the consumer affairs department
contact you. This is a great way to handle necessary direct-dial calls during the day. For every
20-minute coast-to-coast conversation you have
($9.40) for free, the $ is: $9.40

PURCHASES

Buy birthday cards in quantity, not piecemeal.
I've found dime-store boxes of birthday cards (14
for $1.99) are as nice as comparable single greet-
ings (40¢). Not only will you never be at a loss for

a card, but the **$** for getting the box instead of searching 14 times is:

$3.61

BONUS

Install fluorescent lights. They can last seven to ten times longer than incandescents, and since they generate less heat, they're cooler in the summer. True, each costs more than the other bulbs, but you'll benefit with lower utility bills. Should you buy one or more, find out what the electrical savings is during the bulb's lifetime. (The bulb manufacturer should be able to compare the cost of the light versus its utility savings and give you a figure.) It's that number that becomes part of your total.

DAY 23 MINIMUM $: Singles, $13.23; Couples, $13.23; Families, $13.23

Tuesday—Day Twenty-four

FOOD

Select a 3-pound whole chicken over cut-up parts. The butcher can show you how to cut a whole chicken, which usually costs 10¢ less per pound than cut-up parts. That means for a 3-pound buy the **$** is:

$0.30

There's an added savings here if he tells you how to debone the breast. From that tip, you have chicken cutlets at an incredible price.

HOME MAINTENANCE

Drop food coloring in the toilet tank and spot a leak. A teaspoon of food coloring that's put in the toilet tank and shows up an hour later in the bowl signals a leak. Replacing the plunger ball or re-aligning the flushing mechanism yourself (with the help of a fix-it book from the public library) could stop the waste. Based on no more than 1 gallon leaking an hour, you'll lose 24 daily, and 120 ($1.00 per 1000 gallons) in the next five days. Stop it, and the water bill **$** is: $0.12

(See what your plumber would have charged for service and equipment, and incorporate that **$** into your total.)

PURCHASES

Have a free cosmetic make-over. Treat yourself to a department store counter make-over (free) instead of seeing a freelance cosmetician or professional at the beauty salon ($30.00). Don't let "change of face euphoria" pressure you into buying anything. Leave immediately and present yourself to a discount drugstore's cosmetician, who will match the shades with discounted prices or less expensive brands. Since expertise can vary, I'm halving the professional charge, for a **$** of: $15.00

(Your **$** should also reflect what you save on makeup.)

P.S.: This tip is for men, too, as in most make-overs skin treatment is covered, and listen, guys, a little magic never hurts.

BONUS

Try beef-in-a-bag. Processing plants are now shipping a boneless section or subprimal (an en-

tire section of the animal) of beef to the supermarkets in boxes. The beef has been trimmed of
excess fat and then vacuum-packaged in a plastic
bag. Since the meat is boneless, it yields one to
two servings per pound more than traditional
bone-in cuts. Check with your butcher, who will
tell you how to cut the beef and figure your **$**,
which you can then put into the total.

*DAY 24 MINIMUM $: Singles, $15.42; Cou-
ples, $15.42; Families, $15.42*

Wednesday—Day Twenty-five

FOOD

Drink fruit juice that's been frozen. Switching
from a 46-ounce can of grape juice ($1.89) to a 6-
ounce frozen can, which makes 24 ounces of the
same product (55¢), means the **$** is: $0.44

Or:
Substituting a 6-ounce can of frozen orange
juice (61¢) beats a 32-ounce carton of the same
drink ($1.02), because for purchasing the 24-
ounce equivalent, the **$** is: $0.16+

HOME MAINTENANCE

Create your own pest/plant insecticides.

Stale beer (free), placed in a saucer, lures slugs,
which crawl into the brew and drown. Cheaper
than a 3-pound commercial snail killer ($7.99),
for a **$** of: $7.99

Pulverized onion mixed with a like amount of
water (44¢), strained, and put into a sprayer

knocks out aphids and red spiders while beating the cost of a 16-ounce commercial spray ($6.99). That's a **$** of: $6.55 +

Soapy water (1 tablespoon mild soap flakes to a gallon of water: less than ½¢) sprayed on indoor plants handles mites and mealybugs as well as a 16-ounce name-brand insecticide ($6.99) might, and the **$** is: $6.99

(Wash the soapy water off the leaves, and try not to spray it onto the soil. You might cover the dirt with plastic or paper to prevent spillage or contamination.)

PURCHASES
Buy generic drugs and pass up the name brands. You'll do better generically and probably find the alternative to nationally advertised brands as effective. For example:

Item	Generic	Name	The $
20 antihistamine/decongestants	$1.42	$2.81	$1.39
100 acetaminophens (nonacid aspirin)	$1.76	$2.99	$1.23 +
200 analgesics (aspirin)	$1.39	$3.26	$1.87

If you're not sure the product you want is available generically, ask the druggist.

BONUS
Order premiums. I'm always impressed at what various companies offer at very reasonable prices for a proof of product purchase and a couple of dollars. Many of the different items make nice

gifts, so see which ones are being advertised, and if you can use the premium personally or as a present, send for it. Then decide what you've saved and add that number to your total.

DAY 25 MINIMUM $: Singles, $7.94; Couples, $7.94; Families, $7.94

Thursday—Day Twenty-six

FOOD

Select round, not porterhouse steak. Buy a 5-pound round steak, bone-in, 1¼ to 1½ inches thick ($2.30 per pound), as opposed to a total of 5 pounds, 2 ounces of porterhouse steaks, bone-in ($3.46 per pound). It's a **$** of: $8.40

If this buy should seem like a lot of food for your lifestyle, think again. Purchasing larger beef cuts is more economical even if you're single. You can freeze what you don't need, and you won't eat out as often since you'll have more food in stock than usual.

What the butcher should show you is how to cut across the bone end of the round steak so you can remove the bone, the small pieces of meat on either side of it, and the eye section. Take that beef (including the bone) and use it for stew or soup, or have the meat ground. It should yield four servings.

The top round section, the most tender part, can be scored, marinated, and broiled to rare or medium, then carved in thin slices across the grain to give four to six servings.

And finally, the bottom round can be chilled

and cut into thin strips for braising or marinating and stir-frying. Or it could be sliced into two thin steaks, pounded, and braised as for Swiss steaks. Either should yield four servings.

HOME MAINTENANCE

Install a "Bulb Miser." This quarter-sized device fits between the incandescent bulb and lamp socket. It is designed to absorb the thermal shock that a light receives each time it's turned on, which means the filament heats up more slowly to prevent burnout. NASA reports the "Bulb Miser" ($2.95) extends the life of an incandescent light bulb 300%. Based on the cost of a 100-watter (75¢), the $ per bulb with this device is: $0.56

Tot up the $ by:

75% × cost of one 100-watt bulb = $

PURCHASES

Try wallpaper samples as place mats. When you pass a paint or interior decorator's shop, drop in and ask if there are outdated wallpaper sample books available (free). They usually contain a minimum of two dozen sheets, which can be trimmed to the appropriate size table settings. Since many can be wiped clean, especially the vinyl ones, they are reusable. For every package of paper place mats you don't buy (100 for $2.00), the $ is: $2.00+

For each plastic place mat ($1.25) you needn't purchase, the $ is: $1.25

BONUS

Bargain for what you want. In many instances this is possible only with floor samples. But if the salesperson won't come down in price, see if you can't get some extras—free delivery or longer warranty, for example. Whether it's an appliance, apparel, furniture, or a car, go ahead and negotiate. Should you succeed in lowering the cost, add that savings to the total.

DAY 26 MINIMUM $: Singles, $10.96; Couples, $10.96; Families, $10.96

Friday—Day Twenty-seven

FOOD

Enjoy cling, not freestone peaches, with cream you whip. I defy you to taste the difference between cling peaches (16-ounce can: 70¢) and freestone (16-ounce can: 87¢). Although the first is generally used for canning, the second for eating, try the cling, for a $ of: $0.17

Top your savings with a pint of heavy cream ($1.11) you whip yourself, as opposed to the convenience of a 7-ounce aerosol can of whipped cream ($1.19) you squirt, for a $ that's: $0.08

HOME MAINTENANCE

Stuff boots with soda bottles. Closet floors aren't as messy when boots are kept standing upright and in shape with fancy form inserts ($5.00 per pair). But by using the appropriate size empty soda bottles (free), you'll achieve the same neatness and a $, per pair of boots stuffed, of: $5.00

PURCHASES

Serve house brands instead of name-brand liquor.

	Private Brands (1 liter)	National Labels (1 liter)
Scotch	$6.60	$13.04
Bourbon	$6.34	$10.22
Gin	$5.51	$ 6.95
Vodka	$5.18	$ 5.80

If your guests usually choose mixed drinks, it's especially silly to pour costly spirits, because the average liter $ is: $3.10

Should any of your friends prefer their vodka straight, don't be intimidated. Buy a house brand and put it in the freezer. The bottle will be so frosted that your guests will assume the label has more letters on it than are in the Russian alphabet.

ENTERTAINMENT

Schedule games tonight. Ask the guests to bring treats. An evening of board games is a nice alternative to sitting around watching television or making conversation. Suggest that your friends arrive with food: potato chips ($1.03), dip (67¢), beer (6/$2.49), wine (1.5 liters: $4.08), corn chips ($1.12), and soda pop (67.6 ounces: $1.47). Since you have to provide only dessert and coffee and tea, the $ is: $10.86

BONUS

Mix your own dressing, mayonnaise, etc. Flipping through your cookbook will indicate how easy and inexpensive it can be to make your own French dressing, mayonnaise, jelly, and so forth. Many of the ingredients you probably have on hand. For example, mayonnaise is created with egg yolk, hot mustard, salt, cayenne, oil, and lemon juice. Not only do you save money, which you should add to your total, but the food is fresher.

DAY 27 MINIMUM $: Singles, $19.21; Couples, $19.21; Families, $19.21

Saturday—Day Twenty-eight

FOOD

Serve chicken or turkey franks, not meat. As an alternative to all-meat franks ($1.74 per pound), try chicken or turkey dogs ($1.19 per pound), for a per package $ of: $0.55

TRANSPORTATION

Car owners: **Cancel collision insurance or increase your deductible.** This tip is really a special bonus, as it's impossible to relate it to a **$** (there are just too many variables). By the time most cars are six or seven years old, they're worth only their Blue Book value, so consider canceling your collision coverage if you're overinsured. **And** think about raising your deductible as it will lower your semiannual or annual premiums. If you do either or both, increase the diet total by this tip's yields.

HOME MAINTENANCE

Clean with ammonia and water. I've stopped using a nationally advertised 32-ounce all-purpose liquid cleaner ($1.44) in favor of a 32-ounce bottle of ammonia (44¢). Depending on the job (floors, cabinets, walls, etc.), I use the ammonia either full strength or diluted, and it does the trick, while the **$** is: $1.00

PURCHASES

Subscribe to your favorite magazine. Receiving your favorite publication in the mail, as opposed to buying it on the newsstand, is a wise move. Every 30 days a subscription to a fashion periodical means you save $1; a sports review 50¢; a home decorating journal 42¢. That averages out to a monthly **$** of: $0.64

Be sure to see if you can get a better rate than the magazine is offering—through a student discount, an association membership, or a service such as Publishers Clearing House.

ENTERTAINMENT

Screen a movie from the public library. There are 8mm and 16mm films waiting to be loaned, free. If you don't have a projector, why not borrow one, or share the idea with a friend who does? In some instances you can go to the library and reserve a screening booth. The movies include animated features, Abbott and Costello shorts, and Hitchcock classics. Compared to an adult ticket at a revival movie theater ($2.85) as well as a child's admission ($1.90), the library's flicks are a steal. In fact, the single's **$** is: $2.85

The couple's **$** is: $5.70

The family's **$** is: $9.50

BONUS

Appraise it yourself. While you're at the public library, look through the antique directories and evaluate that "special" heirloom or gift. Doing it yourself eliminates the fee a professional would charge (20% of the item's appraised worth). Your $ could be a nice way to top your total.

DAY 28 MINIMUM $: Singles, $5.04; Couples, $7.89; Families, $11.69

WEEK FOUR MINIMUM $:   Singles, $83.86
Couples, $88.50
Families, $94.60

28-DAY MINIMUM $:   Singles, $310.22
Couples, $347.72
Families, $360.75

5

Beyond the 28 Days—More $

Since I believe in greed when it comes to saving money, I've never been content with just reducing my monthly expenses.

If you feel the same way—if you're tired of ending each season with less cash than you planned . . . or following every special occasion in your life with a call for a loan—then I'd like to introduce you to son and daughter of *The Money Diet.* They are the:

5-Day Seasonal Diets (Spring/Summer and Fall/Winter), designed to trim the costs of various items you need during those times of the year, and

5-Day Specialty Diets (Holidays, Birthdays, Weddings, and Grand Occasions), created to cut the charges for those unique events that can empty your pockets as fast as Las Vegas.

80

You might think of these new programs this way: The 28-Day Plan is similar to a basic weight-loss diet; the Seasonal and Specialty schedules are maintenance programs. You see, I'm not only interested in decreasing your expenditures during a four-week period. I'd like to give you suggestions that will help you keep your bills down throughout the year.

Each of these diets uses the techniques of the 28-day program, except they're to be completed in 5 days. To make them any longer would be unnecessary, as their aim is to get you ready for a season or special occasion quickly and easily.

Why not try these plans during the appropriate months or those unique events in your life? The prerequisite for success is a strong ambition to save money and to be good and greedy about it.

6

Seasonal Diets

SPRING/SUMMER

On this 5-day plan, you could save up to:

$485 as a single
$687 as a couple
$723 as a family of four

As with the 28-Day Plan, those numbers are predicated on your following a specific spending program, tabulating your $, and calculating a grand total.

The reason you can realize a larger $ on this diet than during the 28 days is simple: When seasons change you have to spend proportionately more money than you do during a four-week period. There are air conditioners to service, home furnishings to dry clean, apparel to buy. Consequently, my ideas for the Spring/Summer Diet are designed to help you reduce expenses in those major upkeep areas.

Since you'll probably want to begin this diet immediately, let me cover just a few differences between it and the four-week program.

There are two new categories: Health Care, which focuses on ways to shave semiannual medical bills, and Vacation, which replaces the Entertainment section of the 28-Day Plan, as most of us spend our leisure dollars on getting away during this period.

You start the diet on a Monday, not a Sunday, and finish 5 days later on Friday, not 28 days later on a Saturday.

Otherwise, there are no changes. All your old friends are here, from the **$** and **+** to the Bonus and appropriate charts, which can be found in the back of the book following the 28-day diet calendars.

If you haven't been on *The Money Diet* recently, and some of the symbols I've just mentioned are vague, you may wish to review Chapter 3. But if you feel you're ready, let's get going.

Monday—Day One

FOOD

Plant an herb garden on the kitchen sill. Grow chives, coriander, sage, sweet basil, and thyme with seed packets (59¢ each) in large-neck cans, such as old coffee or fruit juice tins (free). You'll also need a 4-pound bag of potting soil ($1.43). Place your garden where there is plenty of sunshine, and be sure to read the instructions on the seed packages. Your yield per packet will probably exceed the contents of a ⅛-ounce bottle of chives ($1.25); 1½-ounce bottle of coriander seeds ($1.25); ½-ounce tin of ground sage ($1.05); ½-ounce tin of sweet basil (89¢); and a 1½-ounce tin of ground thyme ($1.25). That means the $ could be: $1.31

The fresher the herbs the less you'll need for flavoring, so if you're used to commercial varieties, season carefully with your home-grown crops.

TRANSPORTATION
Car owners: **Service your auto's cooling system.** Refer to the owner's manual and do this job yourself. All that's necessary is a "flushing kit" ($1.02), a half gallon of antifreeze ($2.09), and a half gallon of antirust ($5.24). By eliminating the gas station's supplies and labor charge ($20.51), the $ is: $12.16

HOME MAINTENANCE
Maintenance-check the air conditioner. Don't pay a professional to service the window air conditioner ($31.07) or central air-conditioning unit ($34.35). Handle the checkup yourself (free)—the owner's manual tells how: vacuum coils/vents; oil (1¢); replace filter ($1.60 for portables; $1.20 for central air units), etc.—and register, for the window air conditioner, a $ of: $29.46+

For a central air-conditioning unit, a $ that's: $33.14

PURCHASES
Use cornstarch, not baby powder. A 16-ounce box of cornstarch (62¢) is as effective at cooling

feet, hands, and body as a 24-ounce can of baby powder ($3.06). What feels even nicer, the per can $ is:

$2.13

Since drugstores often don't have unit pricing labels, this $ can be found by:

$$\text{your baby powder cost} - \frac{\text{your cornstarch cost}}{\text{size of cornstarch box}} \times \text{size of baby powder can} = \$$$

HEALTH CARE

Exercise with a public library record. Check out a yoga, calisthenics, or aerobic dance disk and start getting your body in shape. (Since untoned-muscle misery loves company, ask friends to work out with you.) By scheduling your own ten-day firming-up session, and not paying commercial rates ($6.03 per class), the $ is:

$60.30

VACATION

Ask for free maps. Borrow a guidebook. Write the convention and visitors' bureaus as well as the highway departments of each state you plan to visit, and request discount sightseeing coupons and maps. Since you won't have to buy a gas station map (60¢), the minimum $ is:

$0.40

(I've deducted 20¢ for postage, but you may get more savings than I in one envelope.)
And:
Borrow a travel guide (free) from the public library instead of buying one ($6.65). Since most

books are loaned for two weeks, you'll be back in
time to return it and realize a **$** of: $6.65

BONUS
   Start a vegetable garden or join a food co-op.
Raise your own produce in the backyard or the
block association's plot. (I read about one couple
who made a $20.00 investment in vegetables and
harvested $300 worth of food.)
   Should you be unable to plant your own, join
or set up a food cooperative. Since you'll be buying in bulk, the prices you pay will make a real
difference.
   A local county extension office (listed in the
phone book under your state's Department of
Agriculture) has information on gardening and
co-oping. Once you're involved, figure the startup
costs and subtract them from what you save. It's
the savings that's added to the seasonal total.

   *DAY 1 MINIMUM $: Singles, $112.41; Cou-
ples, $112.41; Families, $112.41*

Tuesday—Day Two

FOOD
   Substitute mackerel for pink salmon. Make it a
point during the next six months to serve mackerel (15-ounce can: 68¢) rather than pink salmon
(15-ounce can: $2.50) in salads and other dishes.
The change will be refreshing, and for stocking
up with four cans, the **$** could be: $7.28

TRANSPORTATION
   Car owners: **Apply tinted window film.** You can

reduce the sun's glare and heat in the summer by putting on self-adhesive tinted window film. The do-it-yourself kit ($30.00) covers the rear and back windows less expensively than an auto shop's supply and labor charge ($85.00) making the **$**:

$55.00

HOME MAINTENANCE

Clean draperies by the pound, not the pleat. Regular dry cleaners charge per pleat ($1.00), compared with coin-machine establishments that do it by the pound (69¢). For each cleaned pair or panel of draperies—covering a 96x95-inch area, containing a total of ten pleats, and weighing between six and eight pounds—the piecemeal cost ($10.00) versus the machine charge ($4.83) means a **$** of:

$5.17

PURCHASES

Shop the five-and-dime for basics. At the variety store, prices for fill-in seasonal needs are cheaper than at the department store.

	Dime Store	Department Store
Adult cotton jogging shorts	$ 4.30	$13.13
Children's cotton jogging shorts	$ 2.67	$ 8.20
Wide-brimmed adult straw hat	$ 2.93	$ 9.85

The **$**, based on buying one pair of adult shorts: Singles: $8.83

Based on shorts and a hat: Couples: $15.75

Based on two pairs of shorts and a hat: Families: $21.28

HEALTH CARE

Go to the public health clinic and beat physician costs. Your doctor charges for many services that are free through the Department of Health.

	Department of Health	Physician
TB chest X ray	Free	$34.90
TB patch test	Free	$ 7.50
DPT inoculation	Free	$ 8.21
Tetanus inoculation	Free	$ 7.57
Polio inoculation	Free	$ 7.21

Since there are many services you might select, I'm not going to assign a $ to this suggestion, but you can, and it'll increase your seasonal total.

And don't overlook these health care ideas even if you have employee insurance. Your policy may not cover certain preventive medicine measures. Also, why use up your deductible on services that are free or substantially less than your doctor's fees?

VACATION

Exchange your home for lodgings. Swapping houses or apartments through a special membership club ($17.50 annually) lets you stay free at the Joneses' while they live for nothing at your place. That beats the weekly cost of a single hotel/motel room ($29.70) as well as a double hotel/motel accommodation ($54.00). It also means that for a one-week stay, the single's $ is: $190.40

Because they're bunking in the same room, the couple's and family's $ is: $360.50

(If these lodging prices look low, it's because they're averages. In metropolitan areas, for example, you'd add 75% to the room cost, and your $ would be even more.)

BONUS

Alternate a fan with an air conditioner. A 20-inch window fan ($22.50) could help reduce your air-conditioning bills. Using the average .0514¢ kwh charge, a window fan's hourly kwh cost (1.2¢) is cheaper than a portable air conditioner's (4.4¢) or a central air unit's (25.7¢). Should you decide to let a fan do the job periodically, figure its retail price against what you save over the four-month cooling season, and add that number into the diet total.

DAY 2 MINIMUM $: Singles, $266.68; Couples, $443.70; Families, $449.23

Wednesday—Day Three

FOOD

Barbecue with round rather than T-bone steaks. Tenderizing round steak ($2.89 per pound) in a bag for several hours and cooking it on the grill for 30 minutes gives you a delicious and tender meal. I think it rivals a T-bone feast ($4.00 per pound). Freeze 10 pounds of round steak, as opposed to a comparable 11.5 pounds of T-bone meat (you need more because of the bone). Enjoy your buy throughout the season, and even with the marinade ($1.92) the $ registers:
$15.18

TRANSPORTATION

Rent a less than perfect car. There are various agencies now leasing autos by the day ($17.45 with 87½ free miles) and the week ($109.98 with 650 free miles). They're cheaper than those nationwide companies we've known for years that charge daily ($36.98) and weekly ($172.75). The cars rent for less because they are several years old and used, as indicated by the words that show up in the companies' tongue-in-cheek names: Lemon, Wreck, Klunker, and Fractured. Still, you could reduce your rental expenditure by trying one of these firms. If you do, figure the savings into your seasonal total. (There were too many variables dealing with mileage charges and daily rates for us to tabulate a national average **$**.)

Or:

Should you decide to rent from a nationwide firm, fill up *before* you take the car back. (Many of the less than perfect companies don't have pumps, as it's an added expense for them, which they would have to pass on to you.) We found a 19¢ per gallon **$**, because the rental offices charged more for fuel than the gas stations. Based on purchasing 19.6 gallons of gas on the road, the **$** is: $3.72

Don't take out collision or personal injury insurance if you're covered by your employer or your own policy. Decide what you might save daily by avoiding the car agency's coverage, and add that to your seasonal total.

HOME MAINTENANCE

Barbecue with 2½ pounds of charcoal. Make sure you use 2½ pounds of briquets, not 3 to 3½, which often happens if you pour with abandon. Based on a 10-pound bag ($2.09) that gives four fires with 2½ pounds, instead off three with 3¼ pounds, the $, for the two bags you'll probably buy this season, is: $1.05

Figure the $ this way:

$$\frac{\text{your 1-pound bag price}}{\text{number of fires you could get}} \times \left(\begin{array}{c} \text{number of} \\ \text{fires you} \\ \text{could get} \\ \text{in bag} \end{array} - \begin{array}{c} \text{number of} \\ \text{fires you} \\ \text{get in} \\ \text{your bag} \end{array} \right) \times 2 = \$$$

PURCHASES

Make a mothball closet hanger. Three dozen mothballs or 10 ounces of flakes (52¢) in a used nylon stocking can be hung in the closet to do what a 10-ounce mothball brick hanger ($1.55) does. Create two of these devices, and the $ is: $2.06

HEALTH CARE

Get an oral exam at a college. Schedule an appointment at a university dental school. Students, who are skilled and supervised by professors, do X rays, an oral exam, and cleaning for adults ($21.00) and children ($17.00). Stacked against a dentist's charges for adults ($43.00) and children ($27.83), the single's $ is: $22.00

The couple's $ is: $44.00

The family's $ is: $65.66

VACATION

Take writing materials from restaurants/ hotels/motels. As you stop or stay on your trip,

pick up free postcards, not ones you buy (16¢),
and gather stationery (free) to make a box (40
sheets, 20 envelopes: $4.00). (I haven't bought
writing material in years, ever since I heard Viv-
ien Leigh saved money this way.) Based on three
postcards and a half box of writing paper, the **$**
is: $2.48

BONUS

Case army-navy stores. Sporting, camping, and
summer wear that's sturdy, inexpensive, and
often stylish is available at military surplus outlets. Stick with the armed forces issue—tents,
rafts, canteens, fatigues, packs—as some of these
places carry name-brand sporting goods that appear to be at discount but aren't. Tabulate what
you save by not shopping a department or sporting goods store, and add it to the total.

*DAY 3 MINIMUM $: Singles, $46.49; Cou-
ples, $68.49; Families, $90.15*

Thursday—Day Four

FOOD

Buy enriched, not precooked rice. One of the
easiest ways to expand a food budget is with rice.
Choose a 5-pound bag of an enriched brand
($2.89) instead of five or so 14-ounce boxes of a
precooked product ($1.35 each). You need more
of the second variety to get the same amount of
servings. For shelving the larger and perhaps less
convenient food, the **$** is: $3.86

TRANSPORTATION

Car owners: **Turn off the air conditioner.** You

can cut fuel consumption 6% by not air-conditioning while driving the car. For example, on a 30-mile trip, driving 55 mph, you'll save .105 gallon of gas ($1.391 per gallon). That translates to a $ of:

$0.15

(See Calculation 8)
Why save money using this idea only once? Incorporate the tip into your summer driving, and you'll reduce your seasonal fuel costs.

HOME MAINTENANCE

Switch off the stove pilot light. Check with your utility company to see if and how the gas range's pilot light can be put out for the summer. It'll make the kitchen cooler and conserve an average of 400 BTUs per hour ($3.53 per 1 million BTUH). From June 1 through August 30, since you won't be using that gas for a total of 2,160 hours, the $ is:

$3.05

PURCHASES

Donate clothes for a tax deduction. Go through the closets and drawers pulling out what you don't need, can't wear, or have grown to hate. Be merciless. (My motto is: If I haven't used it in a year, good-bye and good luck—the reason I think I lost my first boyfriend.) Take the discards to a charity thrift shop, because, based on:

A single donating six to seven items worth $32.50 and valued at 27% of that by the IRS, the $ is:

$8.78

A couple giving eight articles of clothing worth $36.37, their value figured on the same IRS table, will see a 22% deduction for a $ of:

$8.00

A family that puts 14 items of apparel in a box could realize a donation worth $43.49 and a 22% deductible $ that's: $9.57

Make sure you receive a receipt for the goods' value, and since we figured the percentages on an annual taxable income of $17,000, using the new tax laws, check with the IRS or your accountant for your deductible. Luckily, beginning in 1982, even if you do the short form, you're allowed to count charitable contributions.

HEALTH CARE
Tint prescription eyeglasses. If you need prescription sunglasses consider tinting a pair of your regular lenses ($5.00) instead of buying a special pair for the sun ($45.00). (I didn't figure this idea into the total, since less than half the population wears glasses.)

VACATION
Sightsee on public transportation. A commercial three-hour bus tour of a city ($5.00) usually passes the same sights as a mass transit ride (68¢), and some urban areas have special passes or routes for tourists that are even more thrifty. Using your library guidebook, plus free map and tourist literature, why not explore the city in three hours on two major routes ($1.36)?

That's a single's $ of: $3.64

A couple's $ of: $7.28

A family's $ of: $14.56

BONUS

Go to government auctions. Contact the local post office, police department, Internal Revenue Service office, Small Business Administration agency, and customs service. Each schedules auctions where unclaimed, damaged, or "defaulted" goods (bicycles, televisions, furniture, clothing, etc.) are sold at incredibly low prices. Tabulate what you save at each sell-off, and add the number to your total.

DAY 4 MINIMUM $: Singles, $19.48; Couples, $22.34; Families, $31.19

Friday—Day Five

FOOD

Choose ground beef, not ground round. Hamburgers and summer are synonymous, but there's no reason to pay extra for what you think has less fat when no piece of meat, according to USDA standards, can contain more than 30% fat. That means you should purchase ground beef ($1.34 per pound) as opposed to ground round ($2.36 per pound) and absorb the fat in paper towels once the meat is browned. Stow away 10 pounds of ground beef, not the other, and the $ is: $10.20

TRANSPORTATION

Car owners: **Send the car to auto mechanics class.** Before the high school term is over, take your auto to the teacher, whether you have any problems or not. Let the class look the vehicle over and perhaps suggest and handle repairs. The attention the car will get is better than at a garage, and there should be no charge. Since this one is hard to tack a $ onto, you decide what the $ is, and add it to the total.

HOME MAINTENANCE
Pull the refrigerator plug before you leave. Don't let the fridge run (.0514¢ per kwh) while you're on vacation. Clean it out, and turn it off to reduce the kwh weekly charge on a standard 12.5-cubic-foot model ($1.48) or a frost-free 17.5-cubic-foot unit ($2.22). The $ for being careful about electricity is:

$1.48 +
$2.22

PURCHASES
Plastic produce baskets are good floral frogs. Keep the containers that hold strawberries and cherry tomatoes. (Place them upside down in vases.) They are great for holding flowers and cost nothing, compared to the styrofoam (88¢) and metal ($1.97) devices at the dime store. For using two baskets, the $ is:

$1.76 +
$3.94

HEALTH CARE
Call your doctor rather than visit. During the summer minor accidents or illnesses might be treated on the phone (free) rather than at the office ($26.36). I do it and have successfully reduced my medical bills. Based on just *one* non-visit, the $ is:

$26.36

VACATION
Try mail-order film developing. Drugstores can deliver prints fast, but you pay for it: 12 exposures ($2.66); 20 exposures ($4.14); 24 exposures

($5.31); and 36 exposures ($7.92). Compared to mail order—$2.37, $3.68, $4.47, and $6.66, respectively—the $ based on just 20 prints, is: $0.46

BONUS

Conserve water with special devices. By putting flow restrictors in showers and aerators in faucets you can reduce the amount of water gushing from the pipes without affecting its pressure. These tiny, inexpensive devices (utility companies often offer free flow restrictors to their customers) can conserve thousands of gallons of water annually. If you pay for water, this is a great way to decrease the bill. Should you get your supply free, it's a responsible way to use our environment. So, either figure your $ or take a bow!

DAY 5 MINIMUM $: Singles, $40.26; Couples, $40.26; Families, $40.26

MINIMUM 5-DAY SPRING/SUMMER $:   Singles, $485.32
                                  Couples, $687.20
                                  Families, $723.24

FALL/WINTER

By completing the 5 days of this diet, you could save up to:

$323 if you're single
$374 should you be a couple
$425 if you're a family of four

Again, these $ are based on your finishing a series of recommendations, tabulating your $ for doing those ideas, and finally totaling all your $.

Comparison shoppers will notice that these savings are more in line with those of the 28-Day Plan and behind those of the Spring/Summer program. That's because during the Fall/Winter program, one of the major expenses we have each year, which wasn't featured in the 28-Day Plan but did show up in the Spring/Summer, is finished—the vacation.

If you've done the Spring/Summer Diet, you won't find this 5-day regimen any different, although the Entertainment section has replaced the Vacation classification, for the reason just covered.

Should you not have been on *The Money Diet* for a while, you may wish to review Chapter 3. Otherwise, just begin.

Monday—Day One

FOOD

Serve beef kidney, not stew meat. An alternative to stew meat ($2.27 per pound) in a dish is beef kidney (44¢ per pound), which can make a hearty meal during this upcoming chilly season. (Since you may wish to experiment with kidney, I'm not recommending a bulk buy. You decide what it might be after you taste the switch.) Based on four servings per pound, the individual serving $ is 45.7¢ for a single's $ of: $0.46

A couple's $ of: $0.91

A family's $ of: $1.83

TRANSPORTATION

Car owners: **Repair small body scratches.** A do-it-yourself kit plus sandpaper and paint ($15.00) handles a 6x8-inch area. So do auto repair shops ($68.20), and for not letting them, the $ is: $53.20

HOME MAINTENANCE

Make a kitchen exhaust fan cover and door draft stoppers. You can keep your home warmer with two easily made devices. By flattening an 8-inch or 10-inch baking tin ($1.87) and taping it to the grill plate of the kitchen fan, you won't need to purchase a special cover ($3.50). The $ for making it is: $1.63

(Always remove the tin when using the fan.)
And:

By pushing an area rug up against a door's base, you can stop drafts and eliminate buying one of those special fabric-covered sandbag strips ($9.95 per pair) devised to do the same job. Improvise two makeshift door draft-stoppers, and the $ is: $9.95

(For safety's sake, practice moving the rugs away from the doors so you'll be able to escape quickly should there be a fire.)

PURCHASES

Convert a motheaten sweater into gloves and a hat. It never seems to fail. No matter how careful we are with mothballs, some of those white fluttering devils manage to make a meal of at least one sweater. Why not cut out a ski cap and pair of mittens from the damaged garment? Use an old knit hat and gloves for a pattern and unraveled yarn from the sweater as thread. For each dime-store adult's hat ($3.50) and child's hat ($2.00), and every adult's pair of mittens ($3.00) and child's gloves ($1.29) you design, there's a nice $. Based on one cap and one pair of mittens, the single's and couple's $ is: $6.50

Based on outfitting an adult and child, a family's $ might be: $9.79

HEALTH CARE

Attend charity quit-smoking classes. Local branches of the American Cancer Society and American Lung Association have courses to help you break the cigarette compulsion (some are free; others request a donation: $15.00; a few charge: $25.00). Compared to a commercial class ($320), even if you have to shell out $25.00, the $ is $295.

To be fair to those who don't smoke, I'm not including this in the diet total. But for those of you who'd like to quit, this can be an effective and thrifty way to do it. Should you be successful, increase your total by whatever you didn't spend on a commercial class and what you saved by not purchasing cigarettes for the next six months.

ENTERTAINMENT

Listen to the radio; don't go to the movies. Programs like *Mystery Theater* and National Public Radio's *NPR Playhouse* are just a few of the programs that can be as much fun as a first-run film, where adult's admission ($4.25) and children's tickets ($2.36) are more costly than two hours of radio listening (1¢), based on .0514¢ per kwh. Skip two movies this season and tune in for a single's $ of: $8.48

A couple's $ of: $16.98

A family's $ of: $26.42

BONUS

Sign up for a movie channel. Cable TV now lets you avoid bad weather, long lines, and transportation costs by bringing recent movies, current sporting events, specials, and concerts into your living room or den. I find the monthly investment more than pays for itself, and I'm single. Imagine what you couples and families could save. Should you try one of these services, subtract the installation charge and monthly fees during this fall/winter from what you would have spent to catch the same fare outside the home. That's the figure to add on to the total.

DAY 1 MINIMUM $: Singles, $80.22; Couples, $89.17; Families, $102.82

Tuesday—Day Two

FOOD

Buy a box of potatoes, not a bag. As you stock up on staples, consider a 1-pound box of instant potato mix ($1.49), which contains from 5 to 7 pounds of the vegetable. A 5-pound bag of spuds ($1.98) is just that, and more expensive. Compare the prices, and the $ could be:

$0.49

TRANSPORTATION

Car owners: **Put on a protective wax yourself.** A commercial all-weather protective wax kit ($24.00) helps you get a car ready to face the elements. True, an auto body shop does similar work, but its charge for supplies and labor ($99.42) makes a do-it-yourself job worthwhile, because the $ is:

$75.42

HOME MAINTENANCE

Buy industrial carpet samples rather than doormats. Since this is the season to replace 14x24-

inch door mats ($6.40 each), why not go to that floor-covering outlet where you purchased the carpet samples for your car during the 28-day diet? This time ask for 18x24-inch swatches of heavy-duty industrial carpeting ($2.00 each), which is more resistant to the elements than residential carpeting. Select two swatches and you won't need a pair of expensive doormats. You'll realize a $ of: $8.80

PURCHASES
   Shop mail order instead of department stores. Buying with a catalogue is convenient and thrifty. Since many of us need underwear this time of year, consider ordering it through the mails.

	Mail Order	Department Store
Ladies'	$5.90 (3 pr.)	$2.52 (1 pr.)
Men's	$4.39 (3 pr.)	$8.38 (3 pr.)
Children's	$4.05 (3 pr.)	$5.88 (3 pr.)

Selecting the packages from the catalogue beats a comparable buy from the department store, giving the single a 3-pair $ of: $2.83

A couple a 6-pair $ of: $5.65

A family a 9-pair $ of: $7.48

(I'm not including a postage or handling charge in the catalogue prices because I haven't included gasoline costs to drive to and from a department store.)

HEALTH CARE
   Get a free lab test or do it yourself. How often have you worried about a possible physical ail-

ment until a test indicated you were OK? Why be concerned or spend money when several organizations, such as the American Cancer Society, can direct you to a clinic for a Pap smear (free) or a colon-rectum exam (free); *or* when you can purchase tests at the drugstore, including one to check for pregnancy ($10.56); another for diabetes ($4.06). Lab fees for a Pap smear ($20.17), colon-rectum exam ($35.00), pregnancy test ($13.67), and diabetes test ($10.96) are high. While diagnosis at a clinic is fully reliable, you should be aware that the self-administered tests are only a first step, and if you have the slightest indication of positive results, you should seek immediate professional medical confirmation. Avail yourself of any appropriate examinations or tests, and add the $ to your total.

ENTERTAINMENT

Trade board games with friends. If you're tired of playing the same games, don't let them gather dust in the closet. Swap an adult board game ($9.50) or a child's ($6.00) and the single's or couple's $ is: $9.50

A family's $ is: $15.50

BONUS

Consider nonassembled, unpainted, or mail-order furniture. Shelves, cabinets, occasional tables, and other items that come as kits or unpainted are less expensive than those assembled or stained at a factory. Also, some furniture manufacturers in the High Point–Hickory, N.C., area sell their goods through mail-order catalogues at discount prices. If you're planning to add some furnishings, consider these alternatives before visiting a furniture store. Whatever you save should be applied to your seasonal total.

DAY 2 MINIMUM $: Singles, $97.04; Couples, $99.86; Families, $107.69

Wednesday—Day Three

FOOD
Stock up on mixes to which you add water, not eggs, milk, and oil. Consider those products that need water *only* and you'll probably save money. For example, a 32-ounce box of pancake mix ($1.12) to which you must add 7 cups of milk (96¢), 6 eggs (43¢), ½ cup of oil (23¢), and the entire box's contents to make 87 pancakes actually costs $2.74. A 32-ounce pancake mix ($1.28) to which you add only water makes 48 pancakes. Comparing the two mixes, the per box $ is: $0.23

TRANSPORTATION
Car owners: **Buy a discount store oil filter, not a gas station's.** An oil filter usually must be changed every 3000 miles. Why not select one at a discount store ($2.02) as opposed to the service station ($6.59), for a $ that's: $4.57

HOME MAINTENANCE
Clean your upholstered furniture like a pro. A 16-ounce bottle of upholstery shampoo ($2.25) and a 16-ounce spray can of fabric protector ($4.07), which completes the job and helps upholstery resist soils and stains, can put your love seats and armchairs in shape. A professional will

too, but charge per armchair ($35.04) and per sofa ($66.46).

By using ⅓ bottle of shampoo and 1 can of fabric protector per armchair, the **$** is: $28.18 +

Cleaning with ⅔ bottle of shampoo and 3½ cans of fabric protector per 6-foot sofa, the **$** is: $50.71

PURCHASES

Wash your down or fiber-filled coat. Don't dry clean it. Take a few minutes to hand launder your down or polyester-filled apparel with ¼ cup of a liquid cold water wash (48¢). Then you won't have to dry clean it ($8.50). Per coat, the **$** is: $8.02

HEALTH CARE

Take a free flu shot. A physician charges for flu shots: adults ($9.93) and children ($10.67). The Department of Health offers them without charge. Should you decide you want an inoculation, the single's **$** is: $9.93

A couple's **$** is: $19.86

A family's **$** is: $41.20

ENTERTAINMENT

Buy a subscription ticket. One of the most economical ways to enjoy a play or concert is on a season pass. Here's why:

	Single Adult Admission	Season Adult Admission	Per Ticket $
Play	$10.15	$6.81	$3.34
Concert	$12.93	$9.68	$3.25

Since most seasons feature six programs, the single's $ for seeing as many plays is: $20.04

The couple's $ for similar fare is: $40.08

And the single's $ for attending a half dozen concerts on subscription is: $19.50+

A couple's $ is: $39.00+

BONUS

Develop a skill in the classroom. Adult education courses are offered in many areas, ranging from auto mechanics to calligraphy. Why not study a line of work you can sell after you graduate? Add your equipment and class expense, subtract it from the money you eventually earn, and apply that number to the diet total.

DAY 3 MINIMUM $: Singles, $70.43; Couples, $99.86; Families, $121.20

Thursday—Day Four

FOOD

Serve sirloin lamb chops, not sirloin steak. If you're looking for delicious meat, try sirloin lamb chops, bone-in ($2.69 per pound), not sirloin steak, bone-in ($3.12 per pound). Based on two to two and a half servings per pound, and freezing at least six pounds of lamb, the $ is: $2.58

TRANSPORTATION

Car owners: **Clean the auto's upholstery and interior yourself.** A professional will make your car's interior sparkle ($36.89), but so can you with a 16-ounce bottle of upholstery shampoo ($2.25) and three to four 16-ounce spray cans of fabric protector ($4.07 each). By doing it yourself, the **$** is: $20.40

HOME MAINTENANCE

Borrow what you need. Instead of renting, on a daily basis, a 24-foot extension ladder ($10.00), a ⅜-inch or ¼-inch electric drill ($6.00), a rug shampooer ($10.00), or a quart-sized airless paint sprayer ($23.00), borrow from your friends, neighbors, or the landlord/superintendent. Considering the repairs and cleaning you'll probably be doing, a minimum **$**, based on the drill, is: $6.00

PURCHASES

Make your own fire logs. Why buy a fast-lighting log ($1.00) when your old newspapers can supply the same atmosphere? Roll about two dailies, tie not too snugly with short strings at the center and either end, soak in water overnight (eight hours), and let dry for a couple of weeks. Stockpile ten and consider their worth, half the value of the instant logs for a **$** of: $5.00

(This tip is not for wood-burning stoves. For those of you who heat that way, contact the U.S. Department of Agriculture Forest Service in your area. It may have a program that will entitle you to chop down certain trees on specific tracts of land. And don't overlook lumber yard refuse bins or scrap piles, housing construction sites, trees fell by natural causes, and barter clubs, such as the one you may have contacted in the 28-Day Plan.)

For those of you who don't own fireplaces, do this idea anyway, and give the paper logs to friends as a host or hostess gift. Tied in red ribbon, they're bound to please—and save you the price of a present.

HEALTH CARE

Ask your physician for drug samples. Should you need prescription drugs this season, see if your doctor has samples. You'll decrease your pharmacy bill by the number of tablets he gives you. Based on one of the most prescribed antibiotics, erythromycin (9¢ per pill), an envelope of five is a single's or couple's $ of: $0.45

A family's $ that's: $0.90

(Be careful. You'll make a mistake if you take *only* the sample drugs. True, you may feel better after a few days on them, but unless you follow the doctor's *full* pill prescription, you may not truly get rid of the illness.)

Of course, you can save even more by asking your doctor for the generic equivalent of what he may prescribe.

ENTERTAINMENT

Go on a local tour. Skip the movies. Factories, government offices, police and fire departments, airports, and other community facilities conduct tours. In some instances you'll receive complimentary product samples; in others, valuable information, such as how to survive a fire or prevent robbery. For avoiding the movies, where an adult ticket ($4.25) and a child's admission ($2.36) are more costly than a tour (free), the single's $ is: $4.25

A couple's $ is: $8.50

A family's $ is: $13.22

BONUS

Schedule a garage, tag, or yard sale. Look through your drawers, closets, and storage areas, and pull out what you might be able to sell. Either arrange a sale with friends or give one yourself. (I've passed several on the streets of New York, and they were doing a nice business.) Tabulate how much you make, and add it to your seasonal total.

DAY 4 MINIMUM $: Singles, $38.68; Couples, $42.93; Families, $48.10

Friday—Day Five

FOOD

Discover pork steaks as opposed to pork chops. Talk with your butcher about cooking pork steaks ($1.51 per pound) instead of pork chops ($1.68 per pound). He'll suggest how you can prepare them so the flavor will be enhanced. Then freeze a minimum 6 pounds of the steaks, which give three servings per pound, rather than the chops, which yield only two servings per pound. If you do, the 6-pound $ is: $1.02

TRANSPORTATION

Car owners: **Check your auto's wheel alignment.** A simple test at the gas station will indicate if your wheels are out of alignment. Have them fixed ($23.57) and prorate the cost over 18 months for the six month cost ($7.86), as that's how long most alignments can last. Then during this fall/winter season, you'll be saving .3 mile to the gallon ($1.391 per gallon) or $9.43 on fuel, which gives you a gasoline $ of: $1.57

(See Calculation 2, Example 2, and multiply the savings by 180 days)

HOME MAINTENANCE

Raise your home insurance deductible. Studies indicate that increasing the deductible on your insurance policy from $250 to $500 could mean a reduction in your annual premium, for a $ of: $30.00

PURCHASES

Shop the dime store for hosiery. I don't think you can beat the variety store's prices for pantyhose and socks. For example:

	Five and Dime	*Department Store*
Pantyhose	$1.57	$2.92
Men's dress socks	$1.37	$2.93
Kid's athletic socks	$1.46	$2.34

Why not try the less expensive buys, and stock up on two pairs each, for a single woman's $ of: $2.70

A single man's $ of: $3.12

A couple's $ of: $5.82

A family's 6-pair $ of: $9.34

HEALTH CARE

Write the NIH (National Institutes of Health) for advice. The NIH in Bethesda, Md., is a research agency of the federal government, which supports many research and treatment centers, covering both physical ailments and mental disturbances. By writing the NIH you might receive free advice on an illness or be asked to volunteer as a patient in a study. Since the $ for this has so many variables, decide how much you might realize and add it to the total.

ENTERTAINMENT

Have cocktails at home, not at the restaurant. By drinking before you leave (27¢) you don't have to purchase a cocktail at the restaurant ($2.21). Based on one drink per person, the single's $ is:

$1.94

A couple's $ is:

$3.88

BONUS

Find free or nominal-fee recreational facilities. Instead of joining a health club, see how you can weather the colder season in college, university, high school, and municipal athletic buildings. Decide what you save over the next six months, and add that figure to your total.

DAY 5 MINIMUM $: Singles, $37.44; Couples, $42.29; Families, $45.81

MINIMUM 5-DAY FALL/WINTER $:   Singles, $323.81
Couples, $374.11
Families, $425.62

7

Specialty Diets

"S.O." not only stands for Special Occasions, but sometimes for its financial aftermath: Severely Overspent.

The fear of going broke for an annual event or Rites of Passage can be a phobia of the past with these Specialty Diets. The programs, much like the Seasonal Diets and 28-Day Plan, feature easy-to-follow spending schedules, 5-day charts, and familiar terms and symbols.

You'll find the categories are different. A Gifts section has been added, the Transportation and Bonus areas eliminated, as they're no longer pertinent, and a Decorations series has been substituted for Home Maintenance.

Additionally, the setup is slightly altered. During the five days of each plan, I suggest you focus on one category daily.

For example, on Day One, I list only Food ideas. Now don't panic. Athough there are several tips, you'll probably want to do only a couple to suit the occasion. I say "a couple" because the diets take into consideration many different types of gatherings, and just a few of the ideas in each area may pertain to your event. That means these plans have flexibility and repeatability; those ideas you don't select for one event, you can choose for the next.

Devoting the day to a special section enables you to consolidate your energies. I've always found it's best to deal with one aspect of an occasion at a time rather than all its needs at once. By carefully planning your diet days, you will be able to accomplish what's necessary without running yourself ragged.

Since these diets are based on a series of choices *you* make to cut expenditures, there is no way I can calculate a total for your lifestyle. But I have calculated each suggestion's **$**, which you can use as an incentive. Remember, you'll still have to check prices when you put the recommendations into practice if you're going to accurately figure your **$**.

Because these programs are slightly different from the 28-Day Plan and Seasonal Diets, I'd like to offer a few new Do's and Don'ts.

DO begin the diets four to eight weeks ahead of the event's date, to give yourself plenty of lead time.

DON'T listen to the voice that mutters: SAVE MONEY ON SOMEONE YOU LOVE! WHAT WILL PEOPLE THINK? Tell the mumbler: I CAN CUT COSTS WITHOUT SACRIFICING STYLE AND AFFECTION. GO FIND ANOTHER OCCASION-GIVER TO GUILT-RIDDLE.

DO repeat the diets as often as necessary, and keep a tally of every grand total for reference.

There's no more to it than that—as easy as the other programs, and, I believe, as effective.

THE HOLIDAYS

When Fa-la-la-la becomes Blah-la-la-la, the holidays are usually only half over. That's the reason for this 5-day plan, which will get you comfortably from Thanksgiving to New Year's Eve.

Monday—Day One

FOOD

Don't buy a prebuttered turkey. Baste (14¢) a 12-pound bird (86¢ per pound) yourself rather than buy one that's already buttered ($1.13 per pound). It means a $ of: $3.10

Make your own croutons for stuffing. Why not chop up a thrift bakery's day-old loaf of white bread (46¢) which can yield 720 croutons instead of using the contents of a 6-ounce box of bread croutons (77¢) which I found contained only 310? For every box you don't buy, the $ is: $0.57

Select Grade A, not Grade AA eggs. As you probably know, an egg is judged by its yolk, and those that end up in the center when cracked are considered Grade AA (dozen eggs: 88¢). Grade A (dozen: 85¢) may not be as centered, but they are often cheaper. And this time of year, when you need so many eggs for recipes, who cares where the yolk falls! Purchase two dozen Grade A's, and the $ is: $0.06

Should your grocer only carry one grade of eggs (AA, A, or B), here's a way to make sure you're getting the best buy for your money. According to the U.S. Department of Agriculture:

"Generally speaking, if there is less than a 7 cent price spread per dozen eggs between one size and the next smaller size in the same grade, you'll get more for your money by buying the larger size."

Purchase a canned ham, not a packaged ham, bone-in. You can realize about five servings per pound with a canned ham (5 pounds: $12.50), but only two to three with a bone-in ham ($1.26 per pound). Select a canned version, and the $ is: $0.10

Pack a shopper's lunch rather than buy one. Taking a cue from the 28-Day Plan, why not make your own lunch ($1.29) and a thermos of coffee (8¢ per cup) or tea (7¢ per cup)? That way, you can sit and relax on a shopping mall bench and watch everyone getting holidayitis as they look for gifts, lost children, and a place to eat.

A comparable lunch at a coffee shop ($4.27) means a meal $ of: $2.98

A similar cup of coffee at a counter (37¢) gives a $ of: $0.29

A like cup of tea (37¢) is a $ of: $0.30

Tuesday—Day Two

DECORATIONS

Decorate with what's free or on hand. You could: take a walk through a forest or the park and pick up pine cones; wrap empty boxes in holiday paper and stack on tables; toss greeting cards into a basket, or put Christmas balls in a clear bowl. By being creative, you don't have to buy special centerpieces or table ornaments

($15.00). For each decoration you design, the **$** could be: $15.00

Make your own wreath. When I learned how easy it is to create a 24-inch door wreath, I realized how foolish I'd been buying them. Check the public library for books with assembling instructions, because a similar size evergreen, pine cone, and berry wreath you make ($17.19) beats the florist's ($35.00), and the **$** is: $17.81

Create fill-in tree ornaments, don't buy them. Peanut packing foam strung on thread with a needle (you probably have) instead of a nine-foot commercial popcorn garland ($2.95) means a **$** of: $2.95

A dozen fancy red bows made from a 24-foot roll of 1¼-inch satin ribbon ($1.00), compared to a box of 12 medium-sized Christmas balls ($3.95), is a **$** that's: $2.95

One dozen eatable medium-sized candy canes ($1.20), as opposed to a dozen medium-sized, but assorted, Christmas balls ($5.95), gives a **$** of: $4.75

Buy the tree on December 18. If you must have a real evergreen, don't listen to those people who say you can find a bargain on December 24. All you'll really get is a bunch of twigs. Shop on December 18, when a six-footer ($27.50) will be reduced 10% to 15%, and the **$** could register: $3.44

One way to make an investment in a Christmas tree is to buy one that's ready to be planted (five to six foot: $50.00 to $60.00). A friend of mine did this as a child (the family put the bagged roots in a plastic tub) and remembers fondly that taking down the tree didn't signal the end of anything. It meant another memory added to the yard.

Put the tree in a window and eliminate outside decorations. Instead of stringing exterior lights around the house or apartment windows, stand the tree near the plate glass and use it as a focal point. Not only will the place look less like a roadside diner, but you'll decrease your utility bill. For not burning one 25-foot strand of twenty-five 7-watt bulbs and using 8.4 kwh from December 18 to January 2 (.0514¢ per kwh), the **$** is: $0.43

Wednesday—Day Three

PURCHASES

Send postcard greetings, not boxed cards. Twenty-five cards in a box ($6.40) when stamped first class ($5.00) are more costly to send than twenty holiday postcards from a package ($2.25) with postage ($2.60). When you figure on a per card and stamp basis, the per 20 **$** is: $4.20

Forget a smoker's candle if you're using tapers. Even if you abhor cigarettes, it's not necessary to light a smoker's candle ($2.49) when you're burning tapers. Whether they're 8, 10, or 12 inches, they do the job while giving a **$** of: $2.49

Use products you have; avoid a special spot cleaner. Rather than purchasing a 4-ounce spot remover (75¢) or a 16-ounce concentrated upholstery and rug shampoo ($1.05), handle party spills with club soda, dishwashing liquid and water, even instant shaving lather. Since you probably have them on hand, you eliminate the need to buy special products, and the minimum $ is: $0.75

Substitute a cupcake tin for a cooling rack. Look around your kitchen to decide what can be flipped upside down and utilized as a cooling rack ($3.50). I find cupcake tins fill in nicely when turned over, and at the same time, the $ per rack not purchased is: $3.50

Try dime-store wrap, yarn for ribbon, and pieces of wrapping paper for tags. Gifts don't have to look like a window display. I'm always amazed at what expense some people go to when preparing a present, especially when you think the only thing the recipient wants to do is tear their pretty work to shreds.

This season, why not select a 100-square-foot roll of dime-store holiday paper ($3.50), not fancy wrap on a 50-square-foot roll ($3.75), for a $ of: $4.00

Then intertwine two 3.52-ounce bulky knitting worsted skeins ($2.38; each runs about 130 to 135 yards) for use as ribbon and skip buying a 400-foot multicolored 3/16-inch-wide ribbon ($1.04). That means a $ of: $1.34

Finally, cut a 2-inch rectangle from the wrapping paper, write "To" and "From" on a 1-inch section, fold, and tape to the gift. Not only does the label match the wrap, but you don't need a special tag (10¢ each). Create ten, and the $ is: $1.00

Thursday—Day Four

ENTERTAINMENT

Borrow holiday records from the public library.
Music and story disks from the library can be as
much fun as those you buy ($5.18). For two LPs
you borrow, the **$** is: $10.36

Attend a church or college concert. Getting in
the holiday mood may cost you nothing or a donation ($3.00), but whatever, an event at a cathe-
dral, university, or high school is cheaper than a
commercial activity at the concert hall ($9.50).
The single's **$** is: $6.50

A couple's **$** is: $13.00

A family's **$** is: $32.00

Go caroling rather than to the movies. Since
most of us like to get out at night during the holidays, think about putting a caroling group together or joining one. It's a great way to meet or
see people without having to spend money, for
example at the movies (adult admission: $4.25; a
child's: $2.36). By setting up a singalong, the sin-
gle's **$** is: $4.25

A couple's **$** is: $8.50

A family's **$** is: $13.22

Make your own ice; buy store brand mixers.
For each 5-pound bag of ice (49¢) you don't purchase, because you've made a special effort to
freeze ahead, the **$** is: $0.49

By buying store brand mixers—tonic (52¢),
club soda (48¢), and ginger ale (51¢)—you bypass

119

name brands (at 70¢, 66¢, and 75¢, respectively). That means that by sticking to the 28-ounce store labels, selecting two of each, the $ is: $1.20

Give a Sunday afternoon eggnog and cookie party, not a cocktail affair. Keeping it simple and early is a way to cut your entertainment expenses. For example, a cookie and eggnog "do" ($1.99 per person) is thriftier than a cocktail and hors d'oeuvres party ($2.49 per person). Based on inviting 20 people, the $ is: $10.00

Friday—Day Five

GIFTS

Shop charity and church craft bazaars. Many organizations start making rag dolls, pottery, household accessories, etc., in the summer, so you can reduce gift costs in November. I find I can save 20% to 50% on each craft selected, which makes the average per item $: $3.00

Give essentials as host/hostess gifts. Candy is a lovely present, but let's face it, who really needs or wants any? Consider giving things that are thoughtful and useful—for example, a 10-pound bag of ice (98¢), a half dozen eight-inch candles ($2.88), or four 23-ounce bottles of French mineral water ($3.36). Instead of a 2-pound box of candy ($8.85), select one of these ideas, and the minimum $ for choosing the mineral water over the chocolates is: $5.49

Should you normally buy liquor, the $ is even more.

Wrap lottery tickets. Trying to thank service people such as the doorman and sanitation crew

120

isn't easy. What's worse, it can be very expensive. I reduce the amount of money I give by $5.00 when I include two lottery tickets ($1.00 per ticket) with my greeting card thanks. Whether the numbers win or not, the gift creates quite a stir. After all, you've thought enough to help make the individual a millionaire. For each person you take care of this way, the $ is: $3.00

Put your office friends in pictures. When you can't think what to give those on the job, pack your camera and shoot a series of photos during a break. A dozen color prints (film, flash, and developing: $7.32) can be reviewed, and, say, six put in appropriate size dime store metal frames (89¢ per frame). Instead of spending $5.00 or more on a gift, you've only paid $2.11, and the per present $ is: $2.89

Donate to your boss's charity. Impressing the man or woman you work for isn't easy. At Christmas, unless you shop Tiffany's, it's often impossible. Find out what your employer's favorite charity is and make a donation ($5.00). He or she will receive a card stating you've contributed in his or her name but there will be no indication of the amount. It's a personal present and a tax deduction for you. Based on normally giving an $8.00 gift, the $ is: $3.00

BIRTHDAY PARTIES AND GIFTS

Who said, "When you stop celebrating birthdays, you're no longer living?"

Whoever did never hosted a party or tried to find just the

right gift, but with this Specialty Diet, the anxiety and expense that usually accompany birthdays can be brought under control. Here's how . . .

Monday—Day One

FOOD

Bake, don't buy a cake. Whether you're partying at a restaurant or home, it's less expensive when you make a cake for ten ($3.60, which includes the cost of the ingredients, dime store lettering and candles). Not buying a bakery's version ($10.22) means a $ of: $6.62

Serve ice milk, not ice cream. We suggested this in the 28-Day Plan, but it's worth listing again. A half gallon of ice milk ($1.94) versus the same amount of ice cream ($2.24) gives a per half-gallon $ of: $0.30

Dine at a Chinese restaurant and order less food. Celebrating by eating out isn't too costly if everyone shares the bill, but it's more thrifty for each guest when you select a Chinese restaurant. The reason: Since the portions are always large, you can choose seven dishes even though ten people will be dining. Based on the average entree charge ($5.00), the $ for a host or hostess (as well as for each person) is: $1.50

Ask the guests to bring the food. Why take on the full responsibility of preparing a birthday dinner for ten, when those you've invited might be pleased to help with: hors d'oeuvres (sharp cheddar cheese and crackers: $7.44), wine (two 1.5-liter bottles: $8.16), salad (tossed greens with carrots, celery, and French dressing: $3.26), dinner rolls ($2.68), and a side dish (asparagus: $2.10). That leaves you with making the entree, cake, ice milk, and coffee or tea, and a $ of:

$23.64

Schedule a party without lunch or dinner. Ten adults enjoying cake, a half gallon of ice milk, and wine ($13.70) saves you from creating a chicken dinner with a cake and ice milk chaser ($62.74). The $ is:

$49.04

Use this technique with ten children, serving them cake, a half gallon of ice milk, and fruit juice ($7.18) instead of hot dogs, potato chips, beverage, and dessert ($16.86), for a $ of:

$9.68

Tuesday—Day Two

DECORATIONS

Let guests create the tablecloth. Giving those you've invited some crayons from a box of 24 ($1.15) and showing them the birthday table on which you've placed brown wrapping paper (99¢ a roll) should stimulate their imagination to create a tablecloth. Their greetings and drawings will make the event more personal, and since you don't have to buy a 60x120-inch decorative paper cloth ($2.50), the $ is:

$0.36

Punch out your own confetti. Should you not have a hole punch, simply tear colorful junk mail letters and envelopes as well as magazine covers into tiny strips. Then scatter the pieces like confetti on a tablecloth. Since you won't have to purchase a 5-ounce bag of confetti ($1.10), the $ is:

$1.10

Make a "Happy Birthday" sign. With what's left over from the brown wrapping paper roll after you put it on the table, create a "Happy Birthday" placard. Decorate with crayons, pictures of the guest of honor, and whatever is festive and free. By eliminating the need for a commercial ready-made dime store sign (60¢), the $ is:

$0.60

Use gifts for the centerpiece. As guests bring presents, pile them on the table and you'll avoid having to purchase a special centerpiece ($3.25), for a $ of:

$3.25

Scatter balloons as fill-in decorations. Nothing takes up space like colorful and different shaped balloons (a package of 30: 80¢). Blow them up yourself to save on helium costs, and after you place them around the room you won't need two rolls of crepe paper streamers ($1.10). That means a $ of:

$0.30

Wednesday—Day Three

PURCHASES

Call, don't send invitations. It will probably take no more time to phone your ten guests (6¢ per message unit) than to buy dime-store invitations ($1.43) and mail them ($2.00). The incentive: Calling gives a $ of:

$2.83

Try candy bars, not candy cups. Two six-packs of candy bars ($2.74) let you put one individually wrapped treat (23¢) at each of the ten places. That's compared to mixing the contents of a 1-pound bag of candies ($2.39) and an 8-ounce jar of unsalted peanuts ($1.87) in ten dime-store paper candy cups ($1.08). By using the candy bars the **$** is: $3.04

Allow napkins to double as place cards. Write each guest's name in crayon on his or her paper napkin. That way you don't have to purchase ten place cards (94¢), and the **$** will be: $0.94

Buy favors in bulk, or how-to books. The dime store sells packages of kids' favors (6 for $1.14) and those small adult pocket books (69¢ each) with subjects ranging from exercise to crossword puzzles. Considering the minimum outlay for a toy or gag favor ($1.05 each), the **$** for a party of ten children is: $8.60

For ten adults, the **$** is: $3.60

Wrap gifts and favors in newspaper. Birthday paper (30x70 inches) by the package ($1.80) isn't necessary when you wrap with the Sunday comics or a section of the newspaper (fashions, sports, financial, entertainment, etc.) that represents the birthday person and the guests. Even if you need only one package to handle the main gift and the favors, the **$** is: $1.80

Thursday—Day Four

ENTERTAINMENT

Screen a public library film instead of renting one. You may have to borrow a friend's projector, but it's a wise move, as the public library has comedy shorts, animated features, and full-length film classics (free). For not having to rent a 30-minute short ($20.00), a 15-minute cartoon

($10.50), or a 90-minute motion picture ($86.25), the $ for a child's party is: $30.50

The $ for an adult's affair is: $86.25

See what's free. Attending a concert, movie, sporting event, or exhibit that has no admission charge is thriftier than taking ten adults ($4.25 per ticket) or as many children ($2.36 per ticket) to a first-run film. The children's party $ is: $23.60

The adult's $ is: $42.50

Employ college, not professional talent. The drama and music departments of universities and colleges can put you in touch with a student who for an hour can be puppeteer, clown, magician, actor reading the honored guest's favorite poems and book excerpts, or singalong vocalist. The amateur's charge ($32.50) beats the professional's ($83.00), so the $ is: $50.50

Use the public library's storyteller instead of hiring one. Ask the children's librarian in your area when the next storytelling session is scheduled. If the appearance coincides with your celebration, take the children there, and you don't have to hire that person yourself ($30.00). The $ is: $30.00

Stage your own entertainment. By producing a "This Is Your Life" skit with either the children or adult guests, you can eliminate any college talent charge ($32.50). Let the partyers reminisce about the guest of honor or show their skills. Encourage people to bring pictures, a favorite poem, do a unique dance step, anything that's personal and fun. Everyone should get a good belly laugh, and the host or hostess will wear a nice **$** smile of: $32.50

Friday—Day Five

GIFTS

Shop sales. Even if the party is tomorrow, see what's on special and buy it. You'll probably save 20% or more, whether it's apparel, records, liquor, toys, food, toiletries, or a household item. True, the gift won't be returnable, but select carefully and the celebrant won't even consider an exchange. I'll bet buying on sale reduces your gift costs and establishes a **$** of: $3.00

Give a manicure. One of the nicest luxuries is to have someone do your nails. Why not make an appointment for the birthday person at his or her favorite barber shop or salon to have a manicure ($6.33) on you? It's a personal, pleasurable, unique gift that beats the price of an average present ($10.00) and gives you a **$** of: $3.67

Shower a child with change. Instead of purchasing a toy ($8.00), why not put $5.50 in a fabric drawstring bag you make from scraps around the house? The excitement happens when you fill the bag with pennies, nickels, dimes, and quarters. It'll look like a fortune to a child, and the **$** for you is: $2.50

Design a surprise package that symbolizes the celebrant. Take a tour down the dime-store aisles and select items that represent the birthday person. For examples: *The Tycoon*—a Rolls-Royce key chain, a packet of fake money, a pair of executive socks, a balsa-wood airplane, and a lottery ticket. Or *The Gamester*—playing cards, a crossword puzzle book, a rabbit's foot, and a tiny pinball machine. Stop when you've bought four or five articles and have spent $6.00 on the child, $7.00 on the adult. Wrap each present in the Sunday comics and toss them in a box among crumpled newspapers. That way the recipient will have to rummage around for each gift. Finally, wrap the box. For not purchasing a child's toy ($8.00), the $ is: $2.00

For being creative and avoiding an adult's present ($10.00), the $ is: $3.00

Give a subscription to a kid's magazine or an adult's hometown paper. There may be some of you who are tired of buying expensive toys ($10.00) or apparel ($20.00) as gifts. An answer might be a year's subscription to an educational publication ($8.86) or a hometown newspaper ($12.32).

For giving a child something that he'll enjoy monthly, the $ is: $1.14

And for gifting the adult with fond memories, the $ is: $7.68

WEDDINGS AND OTHER GRAND OCCASIONS

Hosts and hostesses need a good solid week in the intensive care unit budgeted into the cost of weddings and other grand occasions.

Going through one or many of these rites of passage, be it a bar mitzvah or silver anniversary, a wedding or first communion party, can be draining emotionally, physically, and financially. That is unless you consider the next Specialty Diet. It's been created so you can economize without sacrificing your love or diminishing the event.

Monday—Day One

FOOD

Bake the cake; don't buy it. The two major cake mix companies have directions for a multi-tiered cake, which depending on its size offers from 10 to 128 servings. By making your own ($7.60) for 50 servings, you won't have to pay a bakery's price ($67.45), and the $ could be: $59.85

Have the caterer prepare a chicken, not meat entree. You can cut costs ($1.50 per person) by selecting a chicken dish over a meat one. Based on 50 guests, that's a $ of: $75.00

Serve a domestic sparkling wine rather than an imported extra-dry champagne. Caterers recommend allotting a half bottle of the "bubbly" per person at a reception. It's smart to select a bottle of domestic sparkling wine ($12.00) instead of an imported extra-dry champagne ($17.00). Fifty people can be served without sacrificing taste, and you might see a $ that's: $125.00

Ask friends to help you prepare the food; avoid the catering manor. You probably have several buddies who might assist you in cooking and freezing food for the reception. A chicken dinner you prepare ($5.72 per person) versus a catering manor's bill for similar fare ($13.15 per person) means a $ for 50 guests of: $371.50

Schedule a champagne and cake reception in your backyard or the park. Serve an extra-dry imported champagne with a cake you make ($8.65 per person). It's less expensive and not as much work as an at-home party that includes the chicken dinner, champagne, and cake ($14.37 per person); in fact, the **$** for 50 guests is: $286.00

Tuesday—Day Two

DECORATIONS

Shop a flower market, not a florist. Two large bouquets you purchase at a flower distribution center ($30.83 each) are not as costly as two selected from a florist ($34.29 each). Knowing where to buy gives you a **$** of: $6.92

Place candles on the tables, not flowers. Whether you're staging a sit-down dinner or tables where people can mingle and relax, it's cheaper to decorate with 12-inch tapers (57¢ each) than small floral bouquets ($23.57 each). Based on outfitting five tables with flames, not flowers, the **$** is: $115.00

Substitute framed photographs for table decorations. Three snapshots (pulled from a photo album) of the person or couple being honored, put in available or inexpensive metal or wood frames ($4.09 each), create a nostalgic centerpiece. The pictures are bound to cause more memories and talk than a floral bouquet ($23.57). Figure five tables for 50 people that feature the photos instead of the flowers, and the **$** is: $56.50

Let the bridal party carry single roses. Instead of a bridal bouquet ($64.32), hold a single rose

($2.64). If the three bridesmaids follow the leader and skip their bouquets ($30.68 each), the hand-held-flower **$** is: $145.80

You can double the advantage of these single roses by placing them in four borrowed bud vases at the head table. They will be a stark and romantic centerpiece that also eliminates the need to buy a commercial one ($27.14). Since the roses have already paid for themselves, the **$** is: $27.14

Borrow everything. Why be shy, especially when friends probably wouldn't mind lending you tablecloths, silverware, plates, glasses, and so forth? Since your guests aren't all wearing the same thing, why should your tables? For avoiding the rental agency charges for 50 cake plates ($6.25 per 25), 50 champagne glasses ($5.50 per 25), and 50 forks ($3.75 per 25), the **$** for 50 people is: $31.00

Wednesday—Day Three

PURCHASES

Consider mail order, not print shop invitations. Lots of companies advertise in bridal magazines to offer a variety of invitations for many occasions. These mail order houses can design raised-print announcements with a separate reception card ($34.33 per 100). Compared to a printer's charge ($48.96 per 100), the **$** is: $14.63

You'll save even more by including the reception information on the mail order invitation. That move eliminates the need for a separate card ($12.75 per 100), and the **$** is: $12.75

Rent bridal and bridesmaid's gowns. Before spending money on a gown, visit a rental company and look at its bridal gowns ($88.54) and other dresses ($34.50), which can be worn by the mother of the bride. If you purchased either, it would cost $239.58 and $97.50, respectively.

For renting, the bride's $ is: $151.04

The bridesmaids' (figure three) total $ is: $189.00

The $ for the guest of honor's mother is: $63.00

Have friends drive their fancy cars. Why rent a limousine ($55.82 each, based on a two- to three-hour minimum)? Let your pals do the driving in their spiffy autos. Offer to have the vehicles washed professionally ($3.30) and to pay for a tank of gas ($27.24). That way you can enjoy the luxury of a new car without putting up a lot of cash. The $ per auto you don't rent, is: $25.28

Snap the portrait during the ceremony or reception. You'll save time and money by not having the bride, couple, or child photographed at a studio ($65.32). Schedule the picture at the event, where the look can be formal but you don't have to pay studio fees. That gives a $ of: $65.32

Hire college student, not professional, waiters, bartenders, and cleaner-uppers. By contacting a local college's placement bureau (for temporary services), you'll be able to employ students ($4.28 per hour) as opposed to paying professionals ($9.05 per hour). Based on three student helpers for four hours, the $ is: $57.24

Thursday—Day Four

ENTERTAINMENT

Four pieces are better than ten. Initially it may seem like a great idea to present a lot of sound by hiring a ten-piece union band for four hours ($1312.50). By thinking smaller, you may be able to create the same feeling with four union musicians ($496.67), while the $ is: $815.83

Hire a college band, not a union ensemble. Four student music majors may play as well for four hours ($440.00) as a similar group from the union ($496.67). The difference is the $, which hits: $56.67

Select a pianist, not a band. Sometimes all you need is a hint of music. Pianists (union) who sing can offer their talents for four hours ($233.33) less expensively than a union four-piece band ($496.67). That means the $ is: $263.34

Choose a college pianist, not a union's. If a union piano player who sings for four hours ($233.33) is too costly, hire a college student with similar talents ($112.50) and the $ is: $120.83

Play records and forget the band. Gather friends' records and cassette tapes as well as a sound system (free) if you don't have a good one. That's certainly less expensive than renting a four-piece union band ($496.67) for four hours, which means the $ is: $496.67

133

Friday—Day Five

GIFTS

Give a book instead of a bond. There are many special publications ($20.00) that adults or young people will enjoy reading and later use to remember the occasion. For example, there are beautiful art books as well as ones filled with scenic photographs, perhaps of significance to the celebrant(s). You can also find hardcover editions that deal with hobbies, religion, history, and so forth. Since a $50.00 savings bond ($37.50) is more expensive, the $ for presenting a book is: $17.50

Create a memorable gift. There are commercial needlepoint kits ($7.95) that give you a basic picture to fill in and a place on the border to add the couple's or person's name and the occasion's date. When you finish the handwork, you can put it in a 8x10-inch walnut frame ($10.00) also made by you. Compared to the average wedding gift or grand occasion gift ($35.00), the $ is: $17.05

Plant a tree in honor of the event. Select a five- to six-foot branched or whipped (no branches yet) tree ($20.00 to $30.00) from a nursery and wrap it as a gift. Whether you plant it is up to you (which means the tree can be put in a yard or at a special site). The idea is that as the sapling grows, so does the person or the relationship. Considering you'll avoid the average present expense ($35.00) by choosing this idea ($25.00), the $ is: $10.00

Invite an artist to the affair and give the sketch. Visit the local college art department and ask who can draw fast and well. Then check with your hosts to see if he or she can attend the reception to draw the couple or honored guest, not posing, but as each experiences the day. For two hours ($30.00), the artist will cause quite a stir (I bet your present will be the talk of the party), and the finished picture will be the focal point of the event. Since you're not purchasing a standard gift ($35.00), the **$** is: $5.00

(No, I don't think you have to frame it. The idea is so unusual that rolling the paper and tying it with a ribbon is festive enough.)

Select an 8x10-inch decorator frame. There are many lovely frames ($20.25) for all types of personalities and interiors. Choose one that will be suitable for the portrait shot. I usually give this gift. It's one that I've never found returned, and is always on display with a suitable picture when I visit (even unannounced). This alternative to the routine gift ($35.00) means a **$** of: $14.75

A Final Word . . .

As you've read through this book and applied its suggestions to your lifestyle, I'm sure you've found it easier to save money than you had previously thought possible.

I hope you also realize that you no longer have to feel as pressured by inflation or a limited paycheck. Now you can make specific choices that will reduce your expenses because you have the know-how.

The opportunities for cutting monthly, seasonal, and special occasion costs are limitless. I wish you good fortune as you continue to discover personal ways to save money while you spend it.

Should you have a money-saving idea that you'd like to share, send it to me at:

Crown Publishers, Inc.
The Money Diet Department
One Park Avenue
New York, New York 10016

If I use your tip in a new *Money Diet*, I'll forward the book as a gift.
By sending your suggestion, of course, you do give me permission to publish it.

Appendix—Speaking of Calculations

Welcome to a section of the book that will help you calculate a few of the suggestions. I say "a few" because most of the ideas can be figured with simple arithmetic. Others require a brief explanation. To use these easy calculations, just insert your figures and multiply, add, subtract, or divide.

Since most of the examples that follow feature the gasoline tips, you should know that the savings are based upon a car that averages:

14.3 miles per gallon
9,485 miles driven annually
664 gallons of gas consumed yearly
7.78 miles per gallon on short trips (five miles or less)
17.18 miles per gallon on long trips (more than five miles)

The Money Diet

CALCULATION 1

Don't warm up the engine, just start and go (pages 17–18).
Don't leave the engine running when you're out of the car (page 51).

1. .75 ÷ your miles per gallon at 40 mph = fraction of a gallon saved when not idling 1½ minutes
2. Gallons saved by not idling × cost per gallon = money saved by not idling one time
3. Money saved by not idling once × number of times done = your **$**

CALCULATION 2

Using the car improperly can mean you'll get less mpg.

1. $$\frac{\text{your miles per month on long trips}}{\text{your bad mpg at 60 mph}} - \frac{\text{your miles per month on long trips}}{\text{your mpg at 55 mph}} = \text{gallons saved per month by getting better mpg on long trips}$$

2. $$\frac{\text{your miles per month on short trips}}{\text{your bad mpg at 20 mph}} - \frac{\text{your miles per month on short trips}}{\text{your mpg at 30 mph}} = \text{gallons saved per month by getting better mpg on short trips}$$

3. Gallons saved per month on long trips + gallons saved per month on short trips = total gallons saved per month

4. $$\text{Gallons saved per month} \times \frac{\text{number of diet days applied}}{30} = \text{total gallons saved on diet}$$

5. Gallons saved on diet × your cost per gallon of gas = your **$**

Example 1

Mark the speedometer with colored tape at two speeds (page 20).

Assume the standard fuel efficiency is 1 at 55 mph on long trips, 30 mph on short trips. Based on that standard, the fuel efficiency at 60 mph is .944; at 20 mph, .87. Going 60 mph instead of 55 mph on long trips reduces the mpg by 5.6%. Traveling 20 mph instead of 30 mph on short trips reduces the mpg by 13%. Therefore:

17.18 (mpg on long trips) × .944 = 16.22 (the bad mpg on long trips)
7.78 (mpg on short trips) × .87 = 6.77 (the bad mpg on short trips)

Now just follow the five steps of Calculation 2.

Example 2

Remove 100 pounds from your car (page 25).

Driving with 100 pounds of excess weight costs you .5 mpg. Therefore:

17.18 − .5 = 16.68 mpg (the bad mpg on long trips)
7.78 − .5 = 7.28 mpg (the bad mpg on short trips)

Continue with the five steps of Calculation 2.

Example 3

Replace fouled spark plugs (page 30).
One misfiring spark plug can decrease your mpg 7%.

17.18 × .93 = 15.98 mpg (the bad mpg on long trips)
7.78 × .93 = 7.24 mpg (the bad mpg on short trips)

Now use Calculation 2, applying your proper costs as you've done in Examples 1 and 2. To arrive at the correct **$**, you'll also have to figure the spark plug expense: Cost of each spark plug ÷ 270 days of use × 15 diet days

$$\frac{\$1.11}{270} \times 15 = 6¢$$

Then you'll want to subtract that expense from your initial **$**.

Example 4

Inflate your tires to standard (page 32).
For every four pounds each tire is underinflated, the car's mpg is decreased 2%.

17.18 × .98 = 16.84 (the bad mpg on long trips)
7.78 × .98 = 7.62 (the bad mpg on short trips)

Follow Calculation 2 and multiple each tire **$** by 14.

CALCULATION 3

Raise the air-conditioner dial from 72°F/22°C to 78°F/25°C (page 23).
A setting at 72°F instead of 78°F increases the kwh costs 63%.

1. $\dfrac{\text{your AC wattage at 72°F}}{1000}$ × hours used June through September = your kwh used

2. Your kwh used × your cost per kwh = your AC cost at 72°F for four months

3. Your AC cost at 72°F × 1.63 = your AC cost at 78°F

4. Your AC cost at 78°F for four months − your AC cost at 72°F for four months = your savings for four months

5. Total savings ÷ by four months = your **$**

(This calculation is for both portable and central air-conditioning units.)

CALCULATION 4

Unplug your instant-on TV set (page 25).

1. 8760 (hours in a year) − hours per year your TV set is on = hours per year your TV set is off

2. $\dfrac{\text{your TV wattage}}{1000} \times \begin{array}{c}\text{hours per year}\\ \text{your TV set}\\ \text{is off}\end{array} \times \dfrac{1}{5} = \begin{array}{c}\text{kwh}\\ \text{saved}\\ \text{per year}\end{array}$

3. Kwh saved per year ÷ 365 = kwh saved per day

4. Kwh saved per day × your per kwh cost × 26 (diet days left) = your **$**

CALCULATION 5

Drive straight; don't weave (page 35).

1. $\dfrac{\text{your round trip mileage to work}}{\left(\begin{array}{c}\text{your mpg}\\ \text{at 30 mph} - 1.5\end{array}\right)} - \dfrac{\text{your round trip miles to work}}{\begin{array}{c}\text{your mpg}\\ \text{at 30 mph}\end{array}} = \begin{array}{c}\text{gallons saved}\\ \text{per day}\end{array}$

2. Your gallon savings per day × 13 diet days = your gallon savings for 13 days

3. Your gallon savings per 13 days × your gas cost per gallon = your **$**

CALCULATION 6

Bypass road hazards or delays (page 37).
  Having to drive 20 instead of 30 mph reduces mpg by 13%.

1. Your mpg at 30 mph × .87 = your mpg at 20 mph

2. $\dfrac{\text{your short-trip miles}}{\substack{\text{your mpg} \\ \text{at 20 mph}}} - \dfrac{\text{your short-trip miles}}{\substack{\text{your mpg} \\ \text{at 30 mph}}} = \substack{\text{gallons saved} \\ \text{per short trip}}$

3. Gallons saved per short trips × your gas cost per gallon = your **$**

CALCULATION 7

Use a measuring cup (pages 61–62).
  When measuring, use 1¼ cups per wash, not 2 cups

1. $\dfrac{\text{your box's number of washes}}{2} \times \substack{\text{box's} \\ \text{size}} = \substack{\text{number} \\ \text{of washes} \\ \text{you get when} \\ \text{not measuring}}$

2. $\dfrac{\text{your box's cost}}{\substack{\text{number of} \\ \text{washes when} \\ \text{not measuring}}} \times \substack{\text{your box's number} \\ \text{of washes per} \\ \text{the manufacturer,} \\ \text{based on measur-} \\ \text{ing properly}} = \substack{\text{your cost for} \\ \text{unmeasured} \\ \text{washes}}$

3. Your cost of washes when measuring – the cost of your box = your **$**

142

CALCULATION 8

Turn off the car's air conditioner (pages 92–93).

1. $\dfrac{30 \text{ miles}}{\text{your mpg at 55 mph}} =$ gallons consumed on 30-mile trip

2. Gallons consumed on 30-mile trip × .94 = gallons saved

3. Gallons saved × your cost per gallon of gas = your $

DIET CHARTS

28-Day Plan: Week One

The Money Diet

	Sunday	Monday	Tuesday
FOOD	Schedule a smorgasbord dinner with friends. **$**_____	**r** Pack your lunch 4 times. Avoid coffee shop/takeout counters. **$**_____ Let kids eat at school. **$**_____	**r** Don't send out for coffee or tea. Make your own 38 times. **$**_____
TRANSPORTA-TION	**r** Don't warm up the engine 18 times. **$**_____	**r** Mark speedometer with tape at 30 mph/55 mph. **$**_____ **r** Purchase a monthly mass transit pass. **$**_____ **r** Walk 24 times instead of taking mass transit. **$**_____	**r** Remove 100 pounds from your car. **$**_____
HOME MAINTENANCE	**r** Put two empty half-gallon milk cartons in the toilet tank. **$**_____	**r** Don't buy a transfer 24 times. **$**_____ **r** Car-pool and skip the train. **$**_____ **r** Lower thermostat to 65°F. **$**_____ **r** Raise air-conditioner dial to 78°F. **$**_____	**r** Unplug your instant-on TV set. **$**_____
PURCHASES	Snip a facial tissue box in half. **$**_____	Shop discount drugstore not corner pharmacy. **$**_____	**r** Buy in bulk to avoid vending machines and candy counters. **$**_____
ENTERTAIN-MENT	Swap magazines with the smorgasborders. **$**_____ Trade comic books. **$**_____		
BONUS	Have clothing professionally repaired or rebuilt. **$**_____	Change telephone services from untimed to budget or timed. **$**_____	Buy seasonal fruits and vegetables. **$**_____
	Day 1 **$**_____	Day 2 **$**_____	Day 3 **$**_____

Remember to total what you pay for products and services, not what's listed in the book.

28-Day Plan: Week One

Wednesday	Thursday	Friday	Saturday
Jse coupons. Shop ecials. Buy no-me or store ands. $_____	Trim meat costs with the butcher. $_____	r Substitute nutritious treats for snacks. $_____	Eat bacon ends instead of strips. $_____
Replace fouled ark plugs. $_____	r Inflate your tires to standard. $_____	r Drive straight; don't weave. $_____	Bypass road hazards and delays. $_____
Substitute a onge or dishcloth paper towels. $_____	Make window cleaner, don't buy it. $_____	r Run a three-minute shower or three-inch tub on weekends. $_____	Substitute community bulletin boards for the classifieds. $_____
Dilute shampoo d double its use. $_____	r Turn used envelopes into memo pads. $_____	Choose disposable razors, not refills. $_____	Floss with thread. $_____
		Attend a college cultural event. $_____ Let friends baby-sit. $_____	Dial a friend long-distance for laughs. $_____
something to a lector. $_____	Shop sales. $_____	Check utility bills to spot problems. $_____	Watch checkout clerks for mistakes. $_____
y 4 $_____	Day 5 $_____	Day 6 $_____	Day 7 $_____

WEEK ONE TOTAL $_____

28-Day Plan:
Week Two

The Money Diet

	Sunday	Monday	Tuesday
FOOD	Serve ½ gallon of skim milk, not regular; ½ gallon of ice milk, not ice cream. $_____	Shop a thrift bakery. $_____	Select regional and seasonal fresh fish. $_____
TRANSPORTA-TION	Try lower-octane gasoline. $_____	Buy oil at the discount store, not the gas station. $_____	Let rain wash the car. $_____
HOME MAINTENANCE	Snip a friend's plants and skip the dime store's. $_____	Cash in aluminum cans. $_____	Handle multiple light needs with one bulb. $_____
PURCHASES	Use plastic bags instead of disposable gloves. $_____	Report misdialed local calls for credit. $_____	Wear two pantyhose, each one with a good leg. $____ Stock two pairs of the same color socks. $____
ENTERTAIN-MENT	See what's free in the newspaper's "Leisure" section. $_____		
BONUS	Don't buy it! $_____	Get throwaways before the sanitation crew. $_____	Buy slightly damaged goods. $_____

Day 8 $_____   Day 9 $_____   Day 10 $_____

Remember to total what you pay for products and services, not what's listed in the book.

28-Day Plan: Week Two

Wednesday	Thursday	Friday	Saturday
Don't shop on an empty stomach. Don't take the kids to market. $_____	Choose pet food by ingredients rather than by brand name. $_____	Pass over veal cutlets for turkey cutlets. $_____	Substitute chunk light tuna for solid pack. $_____ Use margarine sticks instead of tubs, squeeze bottles, or butter. $_____
Carpet swatches make good car mats. $_____	r Leave the car where it'll spend the night, 6 times. $_____	Eliminate a five-mile drive. $_____	Don't leave the car running while you dash. $_____
Stop a leaky faucet. $_____	Don't replace the ironing board cover; repair it. $_____	Cut steel wool in half to increase the quantity. $_____	Trade services with a friend. $_____
Visit a beauty school instead of a salon. $_____	Make a baking soda and water mouthwash. $_____	Make a dog bone. $_____	Arrange tree branches instead of flowers. $_____
		Shop a paperback exchange. $_____	Invite guests who will bring food. $_____
Take advantage of a friend's "trading up." $_____	Share an item's cost to reduce your investment. $_____	Trade clothing with friends. $_____	Reduce credit card balance to $0.00 and avoid finance charge. $_____
Day 11 $_____	Day 12 $_____	Day 13 $_____	Day 14 $_____

WEEK TWO TOTAL $_____

28-Day Plan:
Week Three

The Money Diet

	Sunday	Monday	Tuesday
FOOD	Picnic at home. Avoid a fast food shop or restaurant. $____	Eat beef rather than calves' liver. $____	Revive stale bread with water. $____
TRANSPORTA-TION	Skip the Sunday drive. $____	r Car-pool for two weeks. $____	
HOME MAINTENANCE	r Run the tap only when necessary. $____	Let mothballs deodorize/repel insects in garbage. $____	r Turn off the lights when not in use. $____
PURCHASES	Squeeze a tube with a can key. $____	Dry clean by the pound, not the garment. $____	Get scrap paper at the printer's. $____
ENTERTAIN-MENT	Follow your newspaper's TV directory, not the newsstand's. $____		
BONUS	Scan the classifieds before paying top dollar. $____	Cancel credit card insurance if you're covered. $____	Go for free financial help. $____

Day 15 $_____   Day 16 $_____   Day 17 $_____

Remember to total what you pay for products and services, not what's listed in the book.

28-Day Plan: Week Three

Wednesday	Thursday	Friday	Saturday
erve lamb blade or ound bone chops, ot loin chops. $____	Make your own breaded fish sticks. $____	Pick: sugarless cereal $____ non-individually packaged oatmeal $____	Buy sugar and flour by the bag and in bulk, rather than by the box or can. $____
			Call ahead for what you need and eliminate a five-mile trip/mass transit ride. $____
Find the phone umber yourself. $____	Deodorize with baking soda. $____	Use a measuring cup. $____	Replace 100-watt bulbs with 50-watt reflectors. $____
Try a disposable pen and forget the refill. $____	Give a frame as a gift. $____	Treasure food containers from supermarket buys. $____	Freeze water into a block of ice for coolers. $____
		Eat breakfast out, not dinner. $____	Use public library's books and records. $____
Rethink food portions. $____	Shop factory outlets. $____	Barter for goods or services. $____	Visit a charity thrift shop for bargains. $____

Day 18 $_____   Day 19 $_____   Day 20 $_____   Day 21 $_____

WEEK THREE TOTAL $_____

28-Day Plan:
Week Four

The Money Diet

	Sunday	Monday	Tuesday
FOOD	Take your refreshments to the movies. $ _____	Purchase bulk, mild, and domestic cheese. $ _____	Select a 3-pound whole chicken rather than cut-up parts. $ _____
TRANSPORTA-TION	Pump your own gas. $ _____	Car-pooling; mass-transit-passing walking goes into its final week. $ _____	
HOME MAINTENANCE	Use hand towels for bathtub window curtains. $ _____	Dial 800, toll-free. $ _____	Drop food coloring in the toilet tank and spot a leak. $ _____
PURCHASES	Put baking soda in footwear instead of odor-killing insoles. $ _____	Buy birthday cards in quantity, not piecemeal. $ _____	Have a free cosmetic make-over $ _____
ENTERTAIN-MENT	See a second-run film. $ _____		
BONUS	Shop with a friend's employee discount. $ _____	Install fluorescent lights. $ _____	Try beef-in-a-bag. $ _____
	Day 22 $ _____	Day 23 $ _____	Day 24 $ _____

Remember to total what you pay for products and services,
not what's listed in the book.

Wednesday	Thursday	Friday	Saturday
ink fruit juice t's been frozen. $_____	Select a 5-pound round steak over porterhouse. $_____	Enjoy cling, not freestone peaches. $_____ Top with whipped heavy cream, not aerosol squirt. $_____	Serve chicken or turkey franks, not meat. $_____
			Cancel collision insurance or increase the deductible. $_____
eate your own t/plant ecticides. $_____	Install a "Bulb Miser." $_____	Stuff boots with soda pop bottles, not boot forms. $_____	Clean with ammonia and water. $_____
y generic drugs l pass up name nds. $_____	Try wallpaper samples as place mats. $_____	Serve house brands instead of name liquor. $_____	Subscribe to your favorite magazine. $_____
		Schedule games tonight. Ask guests to bring treats. $_____	Screen a public library movie or videotape. $_____
ler premiums. $_____	Bargain for what you want. $_____	Mix your own dressing, mayonnaise, etc. $_____	Appraise it yourself. $_____

y 25 $_____   Day 26 $_____   Day 27 $_____   Day 28 $_____

WEEK FOUR TOTAL $_____

Seasonal Diet: Spring/Summer

The Money Diet

	Monday	Tuesday
FOOD	Plant a kitchen-sill herb garden. $_____	Substitute mackerel for pink salmon. $_____
TRANSPORTA-TION	Service your car's cooling system. $_____	Apply tinted window film. $_____
HOME MAINTENANCE	Maintenance-check the air conditioner. $_____	Clean draperies by the pound, not the pleat. $_____
PURCHASES	Use cornstarch, not baby powder. $_____	Shop the five-and-dime for basics. $_____
HEALTH CARE	Exercise with a public library record. $_____	Go to the public health clinic. $_____
VACATION	Ask for free maps. Borrow a guidebook. $_____	Exchange your home for free accommodations. $_____
BONUS	Start a vegetable garden or join a food co-op. $_____	Alternate a fan with the air conditioner. $_____
	Day 1 $_____	Day 2 $_____

Remember to total what you pay for products and services,
not what's listed in the book.

Seasonal Diet: Spring/Summer

Wednesday	Thursday	Friday
arbecue with ound steak, not -bone. $____	Buy enriched, not precooked rice. $____	Choose ground beef, not ground round. $____
ent a less than erfect car. $____	Turn off the air conditioner. $____	Send the car to auto mechanics class. $____
arbecue with 2½ ounds of charcoal. $____	Switch off the stove pilot light. $____	Pull the refrigerator plug before you leave. $____
1ake a mothball oset hanger. $____	Donate clothes for a tax deduction. $____	Plastic produce baskets are good flower frogs. $____
iet an oral exam at college. $____	Tint prescription eyeglasses. $____	Call your doctor rather than visit. $____
ake writing aterials from estaurants/ odgings. $____	Sightsee on public transportation. $____	Try mail-order film developing. $____
ase army-navy ores. $____	Go to government auctions. $____	Conserve water with special devices. $____
ʹay 3 $____	Day 4 $____	Day 5 $____

GRAND TOTAL $____

Seasonal Diet: Fall/Winter

The Money Diet

	Monday	Tuesday
FOOD	Serve beef kidney, not stew meat. $_____	Buy a box of potatoes, not a bag. $_____
TRANSPORTA-TION	Repair small body scratches on car. $_____	Put on a protective wax yourself. $_____
HOME MAINTENANCE	Make a kitchen exhaust fan cover and door draft stoppers. $_____	Buy industrial carpet samples rather than doormats. $_____
PURCHASES	Convert a motheaten sweater into gloves and a hat. $_____	Shop mail order instead of department stores. $_____
HEALTH CARE	Attend charity quit-smoking classes. $_____	Get a free lab test or do it yourself. $_____
ENTERTAIN-MENT	Listen to the radio, don't go to movies. $_____	Trade board games with friends. $_____
BONUS	Sign up for a movie channel. $_____	Consider nonassembled, unpainted, or mail order furniture. $_____

Day 1 $_____   Day 2 $_____

Remember to total what you pay for products and services,
not what's listed in the book.

Seasonal Diet: Fall/Winter

Wednesday	Thursday	Friday
Stock up on mixes to which you add water, not eggs, milk, and oil. $_____	Serve sirloin lamb chops, not sirloin steak. $_____	Discover pork steaks as opposed to pork chops. $_____
Buy a discount store oil filter, not a gas station's. $_____	Clean the upholstery and interior yourself. $_____	Check your auto's wheel alignment. $_____
Clean your upholstered furniture like a pro. $_____	Borrow what you need. $_____	Raise your home insurance deductible. $_____
Wash your down or polyester-filled coat. Don't dry clean it. $_____	Make your own fire logs. $_____	Shop the dime store for hosiery. $_____
Consider a free flu shot. $_____	Ask your physician for drug samples. $_____	Write the National Institutes of Health for advice. $_____
Buy a subscription ticket. $_____	Go on a local tour. Skip the movies. $_____	Have cocktails at home, not at the restaurant. $_____
Develop a skill in the classroom. $_____	Schedule a garage, tag, or yard sale. $_____	Find free or nominal-fee recreational facilities. $_____

Day 3 $_____   Day 4 $_____   Day 5 $_____

GRAND TOTAL $_____

Specialty Diet:
The Holidays

The Money Diet

Monday Food	Tuesday Decorations	Wednesday Purchases
Buy an unbasted turkey not a prebuttered bird. $_____	Decorate with what's free. $_____	Send postcard greetings, not boxed cards. $_____
Make your own croutons for stuffing. $_____	Make your own wreath. $_____	Don't buy a smoker's candle. Use the tapers you're burning. $_____
Select Grade A eggs, not Grade AA. $_____	Create fill-in tree ornaments and skip the commercial ones. $_____	Use products you have, not a special spot cleaner. $_____
Purchase a canned ham instead of one that has the bone in. $_____	Buy the Christmas tree on December 18. $_____	Substitute a cupcake tin for a cooling rack so you won't need to buy one. $_____
Pack a shopper's lunch. $_____	Put the tree in a window and eliminate the need for outside decorative lights. $_____	Try dime-store gift wrap, yarn for ribbon, and wrapping paper for tags. $_____

Day 1 $_____   Day 2 $_____   Day 3 $_____

*Remember to total what you pay for products and services,
not what's listed in the book.*

Specialty Diet: The Holidays

Thursday Entertainment	Friday Gifts
Borrow holiday records from the public library. $_____	Shop charity and church craft bazaars. $_____
Attend a church or college concert. $_____	Give essentials: candles, ice, and mineral water. $_____
Go caroling rather than to the movies. $_____	Wrap lottery tickets as gifts for service people and reduce the cash you usually give them. $_____
Make your own ice; buy store brand mixers. $_____	Put your office friends in pictures by snapping and framing shots. $_____
Give a Sunday afternoon eggnog and cookie party, not a cocktail affair. $_____	Donate to your boss's charity. $_____

Day 4 $_____   Day 5 $_____

RECORD OF SAVINGS
BASED ON THE NEED
TO REPEAT THIS DIET

YEAR	TOTAL
_____	_____
_____	_____
_____	_____
_____	_____
_____	_____
_____	_____

Specialty Diet:
Birthday Parties and Gifts

The Money Diet

Monday Food	Tuesday Decorations	Wednesday Purchases
Bake, don't buy a cake. $_____	Let guests create the tablecloth. $_____	Call, don't send invitations. $_____
Serve ice milk, not ice cream. $_____	Punch out your own confetti. $_____	Try candy bars, not candy cups. $_____
Dine at a Chinese restaurant and order less food. $_____	Make a "Happy Birthday" sign. $_____	Allow napkins to double as place cards. $_____
Ask the guests to bring the food. $_____	Use gifts for the centerpiece. $_____	Buy favors in bulk, or how-to books. $_____
Schedule a party without lunch or dinner. $_____	Scatter balloons as fill-in decorations. $_____	Wrap gifts and favors in newspaper. $_____
Day 1 $_____	Day 2 $_____	Day 3 $_____

Remember to total what you pay for products and services, not what's listed in the book.

Specialty Diet: Birthday Parties and Gifts

Thursday Entertainment	Friday Gifts
Screen a public library film instead of renting one. $_____	Shop sales. $_____
See what's free. $_____	Give a manicure. $_____
Employ college, not professional talent. $_____	Shower a child with change. $_____
Use the public library's storyteller instead of hiring one. $_____	Design a surprise package that symbolizes the celebrant. $_____
Stage your own entertainment. $_____	Give a subscription to a child's magazine or an adult's hometown weekly newspaper. $_____
Day 4 $_____	Day 5 $_____

RECORD OF SAVINGS
BASED ON THE NEED
TO REPEAT THIS DIET

DATE	TOTAL SAVINGS
_____	_____
_____	_____
_____	_____
_____	_____
_____	_____
_____	_____

Specialty Diet:
Weddings and Other Grand Occasions

The Money Diet

Monday Food	Tuesday Decorations	Wednesday Purchases
Bake the cake; don't buy it. $_____	Shop a flower market, not a florist. $_____	Consider mail order not print shop invitations. $_____
Have the caterer prepare a chicken, not meat entree. $_____	Place candles on the table, not flowers. $_____	Rent the bridal and bridesmaids' and mother of the celebrant's dress. $_____
Serve a domestic sparkling wine rather than an imported extra-dry champagne. $_____	Use nostalgic photos as centerpieces. $_____	Have friends drive their fancy cars so you don't have to rent limousines. $_____
Ask friends to help prepare the food; avoid the catering manor. $_____	Let the bride and her party carry single roses, not bouquets. $_____	Have the portrait snapped at the ceremony, not in th photographer's studio. $_____
Schedule a champagne and cake reception in your backyard or the park. $_____	Borrow everything; don't rent. $_____	Hire college students, not professionals, as waiters, bartenders, cleaner-uppers. $_____
Day 1 $_____	Day 2 $_____	Day 3 $_____

Remember to total what you pay for products and services, not what's listed in the book.

	Thursday Entertainment	Friday Gifts
	[F]our pieces are [b]etter than ten, and [c]heaper. $_____	Give a book instead of a savings bond. $_____
	[H]ire a college band, [n]ot a union [e]nsemble. $_____	Create a memorable needlepoint or crewel picture. $_____
	[S]elect a pianist, not [a] band. $_____	Plant a tree in honor of the occasion. $_____
	[C]hoose a college [p]ianist, not a [u]nion's. $_____	Invite an artist to the affair and give the sketch as a gift. $_____
	[P]lay records and [fo]rget the band. $_____	Select an 8x10-inch decorator frame. $_____

[D]ay 4 $_____   Day 5 $_____

RECORD OF SAVINGS
BASED ON THE NEED
TO REPEAT THIS DIET

DATE	TOTAL SAVINGS
_____	_____
_____	_____
_____	_____
_____	_____
_____	_____
_____	_____